COME AND SEE

Catholic Bible Study

Wisdom

(Job, Proverbs, Ecclesiastes, Song of Solomon, Wisdom, Sirach)

by

Most Reverend Jan Liesen, S.S.D.

and

Laurie Watson Manhardt, Ph.D.

i

Emmaus Road Publishing
827 North Fourth Street
Steubenville, OH 43952

All rights reserved. Published in 2009
Printed in the United States of America

Library of Congress Control Number:
ISBN: 978-1-931018-55-5

Cover design and layout by
Jacinta Calcut, Image Graphics & Design, www.image–gd.com

Cover artwork:
Sabine Müller, *Wisdom*

Nihil obstat: Reverend Pablo T. Gadenz, S.T.D., S.T.L., *Censor Librorum*
Imprimatur: Most Reverend John M. Smith, Bishop of Trenton
May 25, 2009

The *nihil obstat* and *imprimatur* are official declarations
that a book is free of doctrinal or moral error.

For additional information on the "Come and See~Catholic Bible Study"
series visit www.CatholicBibleStudy.net

Catholic Bible Study

Wisdom

Introduction

*All wisdom comes from the Lord
and is with him for ever.*
Sirach 1:1

The Wisdom literature of the Bible includes Job, Psalms, Proverbs, Ecclesiastes, the Song of Solomon, Wisdom and Sirach. One distinctive characteristic of all of these books is that they are written in verse, or poetry, rather than in prose.

Wisdom Books in the Old Testament — Both in the Jewish and Christian tradition the books that make up the Old Testament are organized in various blocks. The Jewish Bible is often named *Tanakh*, an acronym made with the beginning characters of the Hebrew names of the three sections of the Hebrew Scriptures: <u>*T*</u>*orah* (the Law), <u>*N*</u>*ebî'îm* (the Prophets), and <u>**K**</u>**etubîm** (the Writings).

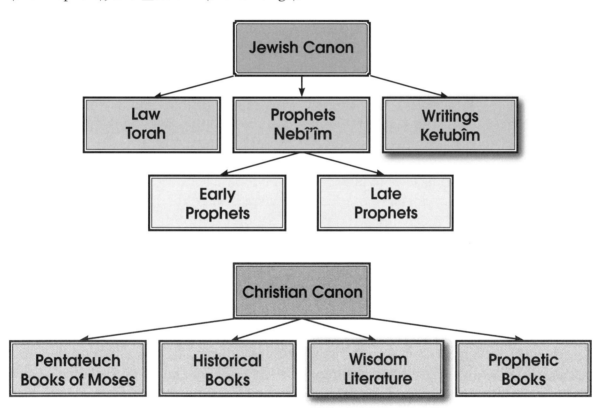

While the Torah and the Prophets were well established collections of books by the beginning of the second century BC, the precise extent of the Writings was still somewhat flexible and subject to change and growth. Growth occurred in the two geographical areas where Judaism was alive and flourishing, Israel and Egypt. The fact that the list of approved books in Judaism was not yet fixed at the time when Jesus Christ founded the Church, has been the cause of much confusion and is essentially at the root of the differences between Catholic and Protestant Bibles.

Two Languages — After the Babylonian exile, Biblical Hebrew was no longer spoken. The text of the Old Testament was made accessible for the Aramaic speaking Jews through the work of scribes who translated the readings into Aramaic (see Nehemiah 8:7-8). This work later crystallized into what is now known as the *Targum*, an Aramaic version that both paraphrased and explained the Old Testament. For the Greek speaking Jews a translation was made available that became known as the Septuagint. The meaning of this name is explained in the *Letter of Aristeas*, a Jewish document from around 200 BC, which reports that at the request of the Egyptian ruler 72 scribes from Jerusalem (six from each tribe) independently translated the Law in 72 days and were then found to have made a very accurate translation. The translation was adopted by the Greek-speaking Jews. Subsequent retellings of the tale mention the entire Hebrew Bible and report that the translators miraculously produced 70 times exactly the same translation (hence *Septuagint* = "70"), which proved beyond doubt that the Greek text was divinely inspired and carried the same authority as the Hebrew text, even though the translation was not always literal nor always made from the same version of the Hebrew books that were in use in Israel.

While the sections of books in the Hebrew tradition follow an actual chronological order, those of the Septuagint reflect a supposed chronological order, in which prophetic books come last because they concern the future.

Two Canons — Both within the Aramaic speaking Jewish community of Israel and within the Greek speaking Jewish community in the diaspora new books were written that achieved the same status as the books in the canon (list of approved books). In fact, there came to be two canons in Judaism at that time: a shorter Hebrew list in use by the Aramaic speaking Jews living in Israel, and a longer Greek list in use by Greek speaking Jews living in the diaspora (mainly Egypt). Since the Law and the Prophets were well established collections, the differences occurred only in the section of the Writings. Eventually, the Greek Old Testament, though an entirely Jewish work, did not contain the same number of books as the list of Hebrew books. This was not felt as a problem in Judaism since, for one thing, in Israel the canon was not yet definite.

All of that changed towards the end of the first century AD. While Jews were deprived of the Temple (destroyed by the Romans in 70 AD) and banned from entering Jerusalem, Christianity was taking shape within Judaism. In this situation Judaism needed to reformulate itself and distinguish itself from upcoming Christianity. It did so by concentrating on the sacred text according to the shorter Hebrew canon. This consolidating process, later known as the *Synod of Javne* (Jamnia), was finished around 100 AD. This new Jewish canon, which is the normative list for Judaism until today, contains twenty-four, twenty-two or twenty-seven books, depending on how the number of characters in the Hebrew alphabet is counted.

The first Christians, who were nearly all of Jewish descent and *Aramaic speaking,* used the canon that was in use in Israel before the synod of Javne. It contained at least one more Hebrew book that Rabbis left out of the later Jewish canon, namely the *Wisdom of Jesus ben Sira.* These first generation Christians were soon outnumbered by the Greek speaking Christians, who got used to reading the sacred books according to the Greek canon of Egyptian Jewry, which contained about thirty-five books. The difference with the Hebrew canon is less dramatic than the numbers suggest. The twelve minor prophets are counted as one book in Judaism.

The important fact here is that the canon of the Hebrew Bible is essentially a late first-century document that comes chronologically after the foundation of the Church by Jesus Christ, who already had inherited the Greek canon. In the sixteenth century AD Martin Luther decided on the shorter Hebrew list of books of the Old Testament and deprived the protestant churches of a number of books that were later called "deuterocanonical" (secondarily canonical) as if they were added to an original list. In fact, however, the canon of the Old Testament used in the Church from the first century AD onwards is more original and predates that of the synod of Javne. The deuterocanonical books are: Judith, Tobit, 1, and 2 Maccabees, Wisdom of Solomon, Sirach, Baruch, parts of Daniel and parts of Esther.

The "Writings" in the Jewish tradition contain the following books: Psalms, Job, Proverbs, Ruth, Song of Solomon, Ecclesiastes, Lamentations, Esther, Daniel, Ezra, Nehemiah, 1 and 2 Chronicles. The wisdom books among these are:

English Name	*Hebrew Name*	*Latin Name*
Psalms	Tehillim	Psalmi
Job	'Iyob	Hiob
Proverbs	Mishle Shlemo	Proverbia
Song of Solomon	Shir haShîrîm	Canticum
Preacher	Qohelet	Ecclesiastes

In its section of poetical books the Greek canon also has the following books:

English Name	*Greek Name*	*Latin Name*
Wisdom of Solomon	Sofia Solomon	Sapientia Salomonis
Wisdom of Jesus ben Sira	Sofia …	Ecclesiasticus

The Wisdom of Solomon was written in Greek in Egypt sometime between 200 and 50 BC. Sirach is an original Hebrew book, written in Jerusalem around 195 BC, translated into Greek around 132 BC and rejected by the rabbis at the end of the 1st century AD. Chronologically the Wisdom books run through the whole history of the Old Testament.

Some date back to the time of David and Solomon and their royal scribes (tenth century BC). Some are as recent as the second century BC.

A formal characteristic of both the Hebrew and Greek wisdom books is that they are composed in verse. A further typical peculiarity of wisdom literature is its predilection for the alphabetic pattern: in Wisdom books there is a notable tendency to articulate the message in twenty-two verses or strophes each beginning with one of the twenty-two characters of the Hebrew alphabet. This stylistic device denotes both completeness and order and expresses something which all wisdom writings have in common, which pertains more to the content than to the form. This can be described as a wisdom outlook on God, the world, and man.

Wisdom Outlook — A common way to understand the Old Testament is to see it as a reflection of the insight which the Jewish people have of their own history. Such apprehension effectively implies that the meaning of the text can only be understood against the backdrop of that history. Within this historical-critical outlook on the Bible, however, there is hardly any place for wisdom literature. A typical feature of the wisdom texts is namely that they do not deal with Israel and its national history: election, promise, Law, and covenant are hardly mentioned.

Perhaps the most characteristic element of wisdom texts is the integrated outlook on mankind and the world. In wisdom books there is a fundamental conviction that there is a right, correct, "wise" way of doing things and that one should search for that and live accordingly. This wisdom is not found primarily in history but rather in all created reality. There is a *sapiential* (wisdom) interest in history only in so far as it demonstrates certain constant patterns, which reveal the way that leads to God. Wisdom teachers extract generally applicable sayings from the sequence of acting persons and of events that constitute history.

Nature and everyday life are more common fields of wisdom observations than history. It is not that the lessons of history are not appreciated, but there is a stronger awareness of the insufficiency of sequential realities to explain themselves. In the endlessly changing sea of time there appear to be different currents and tidal patterns, but they do not carry their reasonability within themselves: the cogency of the interrelatedness of events depends on a coherence which itself is not an historical event. To understand and react responsibly to this identity within all changeability, wisdom looks for natural laws and principles rather than for accurate historical overviews. In doing so wisdom literature focuses attention not on chronology, but on protology, or on what comes first, "(in) the beginning," at the time of creation with all that it entails. Protology attempts to describe the coherence which is behind historical events; it is an *a priori* condition, which enables the ordering of all possible historical events.

Wisdom literature then tries to bring into focus the conditions that render everyday life possible. Everyday life is experienced as a simultaneity of many factors. History describes these elements in chronological sequence; wisdom moves beyond history to a timeless description of what constitutes reality at the time of creation, "in the beginning" when humans were created in the image of God.

The emphasis on the art of living wisely and the attention on practical wisdom leaves one to wonder: where does God come in? For the wisdom teachers of the Old Testament God is self evident: when they speak of wisdom it is always within the horizon of Him who alone is wise (Sirach 1:8). God not only is the source of all that is wise, but also the limit for which all human wisdom comes to a full stop: *No wisdom, no understanding, no counsel, can avail against the Lord* (Proverbs 21:30). A truly wise person knows that human experiences, which sometimes are so conflicting in their immediateness, can have a revelatory meaning because God created the whole world well and gave mankind the task to be good caretakers of creation (Sirach 17:2-10). Biblical Wisdom then is preoccupied with things of this world. It tries to make sense of a complex and ambiguous reality with the confidence that it is not only possible but also a God-given task. The wisdom of the Bible reads today's history in the double light of man's experience and of faith in God, knowing that the latter does not supersede but illuminates the former.

In discussions with contemporaries Jesus is known to consider ethical questions from the "wisdom point of view" of the good beginning which God created (Mark 10:2-9). Since Jesus was well versed in the Wisdom literature, His disciples will also want to study the Wisdom literature of the Bible carefully as well.

Sharing God's Wisdom

Wisdom is a sharing in God's ability to see and judge things as they really are. God reveals himself as God by his just judgments; as God, he sees things without disguise, as they really are, and deals with each according to his truth. Wisdom is a sharing in God's way of seeing reality.

But there are, obviously, certain preconditions to this knowing from God's perspective. We cannot possess it unless we are united with God. This in turn, means that this last and deepest mode of knowledge is not just an intellectual experience. In all that is essential, knowledge and life are inseparable. If something of the incorruptibility of God himself belongs to this deepest kind of knowledge, then there belongs to it also that purity of the "I" without which man is not incorruptible. From this, the meaning of the concepts "gifts of God" and "sharing in God's way of thinking" also becomes clear.

Only if we let ourselves be cleansed of the corruptibility of the "I" and come thus gradually to live by God, to be united with God, do we come to a true inner freedom of judgment, to a fearless independence of thinking and deciding, that no longer cares about the approval or disapproval of others but clings to the truth. Such a purification is always a process of opening oneself and, at the same time, of receiving oneself. It cannot take place without the suffering of the vine that is pruned. But it makes possible the only form of power that leads, not to slavery, but to freedom.

Pope Benedict XVI (Cardinal Ratzinger), *Principles of Catholic Theology* (San Francisco: Ignatius Press, 1987), p. 357.

What You Need to Do this Bible Study

To do this Bible Study, you need a Catholic Bible, and a *Catechism of the Catholic Church* (CCC). When choosing a Bible, remember that the Catholic Bible contains seventy-three books. If you find Sirach and Tobit in your Bible's table of contents, you have a complete Catholic Bible. The Council of Hippo approved these seventy-three books in AD 393, and this has remained the official canon of Sacred Scripture since the Fourth Century. The Council of Trent in AD 1545 authoritatively reaffirmed these divinely inspired books for inclusion in the canon of the Bible. The Douay-Rheims, one of the first English translations of the Catholic Bible, was completed in AD 1609.

For Bible study purposes, choose a word-for-word, literal translation rather than a paraphrase. Some excellent translations are the Revised Standard Version Catholic Edition (RSVCE), the Jerusalem Bible (JB), and the New American Bible (NAB). For this Bible study, the RSVCE second edition by Ignatius Press is recommended.

How To Do This Bible Study

1. Pray to the Holy Spirit to enlighten your mind and spirit.
2. Read the Bible passages for the first chapter.
3. Read the commentary in this book.
4. Use your Bible and Catechism to write answers to the home study questions.
5. Find a small group and share your answers aloud on those questions.
6. Watch the videotape lecture that goes with this study.
7. End with a short wrap-up lecture and/or prayer.

Invite and Welcome Priests and Religious

Ask for the blessing of your pastor before you begin. Invite your pastor, associate pastor, deacon, visiting priests, and religious sisters to participate in Bible study. Invite priests and religious to come and pray with the Bible study members, periodically answer questions from the question box, or give a wrap-up lecture. Accept whatever they can offer to the Bible study. However, don't expect or demand anything from them. Appreciate that the clergy are very busy and don't add additional burdens on them. Accept with gratitude whatever is offered.

Practical Needs

❊ Ask God for wisdom about whom to study with, where, and when to meet.

❊ Gather a small prayer group to pray for your Bible study and your specific needs. Pray to discern God's will in your particular situation.

❊ Show this book to your pastor and ask for his approval and direction.

❊ Choose a day of the week and time to meet.

❊ Invite neighbors and friends to a "Get Acquainted Coffee" to find out who will make a commitment to meet for 60 to 90 minutes each week for Bible study.

❊ Find an appropriate location. Start in someone's home or in the parish hall if the space is available and the pastor will allow it.

❊ Hire a babysitter for mothers with young children and share the cost amongst everyone, or find some volunteers to provide childcare.

❊ Consider a cooperative arrangement, in which women take turns caring for the children. All women, even grandmothers and women without children, should take turns, serving the children as an offering to God.

Pray that God will anoint specific people to lead your study. Faithful, practicing Catholics are needed to fill the following positions:

❊ **Teachers** — take responsibility to read commentaries and prepare a fifteen to twenty minute wrap-up lecture after the small group discussion and video.

❊ **Song Leaders** — lead everyone in singing a short hymn to begin Bible study.

❊ **Prayer Leaders** — open Bible study with a short prayer.

❊ **Children's Teachers** — teach the young children who come to Bible study.

❊ **Coordinators** — communicate with parish personnel about needs for rooms, microphones, and video equipment. Make sure rooms are left in good shape.

❊ **Small Group Facilitators** will be needed for each small group. Try to enlist two mature Catholics who are good listeners to serve together as co-leaders for each small group and share the following responsibilities:

❖ Pray for each member of your small group every day.

❖ Make a nametag for each member of the group.

❖ Meet before the study to pray with other leaders.

❖ Discuss all the questions in the lesson each week.

❖ Begin and end on time.

❖ Make sure that each person in the group shares each week. Ask each person to read a question and have the first chance to answer it.

❖ In the discussion group go around in a circle, so that each person can look forward to his or her turn to read a question. After reading the question, the reader can answer the question or pass, and then others can feel free to add additional comments.

❖ Make sure that no one person dominates the discussion, including you!

❖ Keep the discussion positive and focused on the week's lesson.

❖ Speak kindly and charitably. Steer conversation away from any negative or uncharitable speech, gossip, or griping. Don't badmouth anyone or any church.

❖ Listen well! Keep your ears open and your eyes on the person speaking.

❖ Give your full attention to the one speaking. Be comfortable with silence. Be patient. Encourage quieter people to share first. Ask questions.

❖ If questions, misunderstandings, or disagreements arise, refer them to the question box for a teacher to research or the parish priest to answer later.

❖ Arrange for a social activity each month.

Logistical Considerations

✳ Jesus chose a group of twelve apostles. So, perhaps twelve or thirteen people make the best small groups. When you get too many, break into two groups.

✳ A group of teenagers or a young adult group could be facilitated by the parish priest or a young adult leader.

✳ Men share best with men and women with women. If you have a mixed Bible study, organize separate men's groups led by men and women's groups led by women. In mixed groups, some people tend to remain silent.

✳ Offer a married couples' group, if two married couples are willing to lead the group. Each person should have his or her own book.

✳ Sit next to the most talkative person in the group and across from the quietest. Use eye contact to affirm and encourage quieter people to speak up. Serve everyone and hear from everyone.

✳ Listening in Bible study is just as important as talking. Evaluate each week. Did everyone share? Am I a good listener? Did I really hear what others shared? Was I attentive or distracted? Did I affirm others? Did I talk too much?

✳ Share the overall goal aloud with all of the members of the group. We want to hear from each person in the group, sharing aloud each time the group meets.

✳ Make sure that people share answers only on those questions on which they have written down answers. Don't just share off the top of your head. Really study.

✳ Consider a nursing mothers' group in which mothers can bring their infants and hold them while sharing their home study questions.

✳ Family groups can work together on a family Bible study night, reading the commentary and scriptures aloud and helping one another to find answers in the Bible and Catechism.

✳ Parents or older siblings can read to young children and help the youngsters to do the crafts in the children's Bible study book.

Social Activities

God has created us as social creatures, needing to relate communally. Large parishes make it difficult for people to get to know one another. Some people can belong to a parish for years without getting to know others. Newcomers may never get noticed and welcomed. Bible study offers an opportunity for spiritual nourishment as well as inclusion and hospitality. Occasional social activities are recommended in this book. These socials are simple, fun, and easy. In planning your social activities be a good sport and try to attend with your group.

✳ Agree on a time when most of the group can meet. This could be right before or after Bible study or a different day of the week, perhaps even Saturday morning.

✳ Invite people to come to your home for the social time. Jesus was comfortable visiting the homes of the rich and the poor. So, whatever your circumstances, as a Christian you can offer hospitality to those God sends along your way.

> *Do not neglect to show hospitality to strangers,*
> *for thereby some have entertained angels unawares.*
> *(Hebrews 13:2)*

✳ Keep it simple! Just a beverage and cookies work well. Simplicity blesses others. People can squeeze together on a sofa or stand around the kitchen. Don't fuss.

✳ Help the group leader. If Bible study meets in someone's home, invite the group to come to your place for the social time. Don't make the group leader do it all.

✳ If Bible study meets at church, don't have all of the socials at church as well. Try to have some fellowship times in people's homes. Perhaps over the Christmas break you can go to someone's home for coffee and cookies after Christmas and before Bible study starts up again.

Suggested Times for Socials

9:30–10:30 a.m.	Saturday coffee	12:00–1:00 p.m.	Luncheon
3:00–4:00 p.m.	Afternoon tea	8:00–9:00 p.m.	Dessert

Modify times to meet your specific needs. If your parish has Saturday morning Mass at 9:00 a.m., adjust the time of your social to accommodate those members of the group who would like to attend Mass and need some time to get to the social. If lunch after Bible study makes too long of a day for children who need naps, plan the social for a different day. A mother's group might meet after school when high school students are available to baby-sit.

Class Schedule

Accept responsibility for being a good steward of time. God gives each of us twenty-four hours every day. If Bible study starts or ends late, busy people may drop out. Late starts punish the prompt and encourage tardiness. Be a good steward of time. Begin and end Bible study with prayer at the agreed upon time. If people consistently arrive late or leave early, investigate whether you have chosen the best time for most people. You may have a conflict with the school bus schedule or the parish Mass schedule. Perhaps beginning a few minutes earlier or later could be a service to those mothers who need to pick up children from school.

Possible Bible Study Class Schedules

MORNING CLASS

9:30 a.m.	Welcome, song, prayer
9:40 a.m.	Video
9:55 a.m.	Small group discussion
10:40 a.m.	Wrap-up lecture and prayer

AFTERNOON CLASS

1:00 p.m.	Welcome, song, prayer
1:10 p.m.	Small group discussion
1:55 p.m.	Video
2:10 p.m.	Wrap-up lecture and prayer

EVENING CLASS

7:30 p.m.	Welcome, song, prayer
7:40 p.m.	Small group discussion
8:25 p.m.	Video
8:40 p.m.	Wrap-up lecture and prayer

As you can see, the video could be shown either before or after the small group discussion, and either before, after, or instead of a wrap-up lecture. Whether or not you choose to use the videotapes, please begin and end with prayer.

Wrap-Up Lecture

Additional information is offered in videotaped lectures, which are available for this study and can be obtained from Emmaus Road Publishing Company, 827 North Fourth Street, Steubenville, Ohio, 43952. You can obtain DVDs or videocassettes of these lectures by going to www.emmausroad.org on the Internet or by calling 1-800-398-5470. Videotaped lectures may be used in addition to, or in place of a wrap-up lecture, depending on your needs.

When offering a closing lecture, the presenter should spend extra time in prayer and study to prepare a good, sound lecture. The lecturer should consult several Catholic Bible study commentaries and prepare a cohesive, orthodox lecture. Several members of the leaders' team could take turns giving wrap-up lectures. Also, invite priests, deacons, and religious sisters to give an occasional lecture.

The lecturer should:
* Be a faithful, practicing Catholic. Seek spiritual direction. Frequent the sacraments, especially the Eucharist and Reconciliation.
* Obtain the approval and blessing of your parish priest to teach.
* Use several different presenters whenever possible.
* Pray daily for all of the leaders and members of the study.
* Pray over the lesson to be studied and presented.

* Outline the Bible passages to be studied.
* Identify the main idea of the Bible study lesson.
* Find a personal application from the lesson. How can one make a practical response to God's word?
* Plan a wrap-up lecture with a beginning, a middle, and an end.
* Use index cards to keep focused. Don't read your lecture; talk to people.

* Proclaim, teach, and reiterate the teachings of the Catholic Church. Learn what the Catholic Church teaches, and proclaim the fullness of truth.
* Illustrate the main idea presented in the passage by using true stories from the lives of the saints, or the lives of contemporary Christians.
* Use visuals—a flip chart or overhead transparencies if possible.
* Plan a skit, act out a Bible story, and interact with the group.

* Try to make the scriptures come alive for the people in your group.
* Provide a question box. Find answers to difficult questions or ask a parish priest to come and answer questions on occasion.
* When difficult or complex personal problems arise or are shared in the group, seek out the counsel of a priest.
* Begin and end on time. When you get to the end of your talk, stop and pray.

Challenges

"All scripture is inspired by God and profitable for teaching, for reproof, for correction, and for training in righteousness, that the man of God may be complete, equipped for every good work" (2 Timothy 3:16-17).

As Christians, all of us are weak and need God's mercy and forgiveness. Lay groups can attract people with problems and challenges. Don't try to be all things for all people. Jesus is the Savior, and we are only His servants. When problems loom, direct them to a priest or counselor. Bible study demands faithfulness to the one task at hand, while praying for others in their needs. Saint Paul encourages us to "speak the truth in love… and be kind to one another, tenderhearted, forgiving one another, as God in Christ forgave you" (Ephesians 4:15,32). Bible study provides the opportunity for us to search God's word for direction in our personal lives and to pray for, encourage, and sometimes gently admonish one another.

"Seek then the highest wisdom, not by arguments in words but by the perfection of your life, not by speech but by the faith that comes from simplicity of heart, not from the learned speculations of the unrighteous. If you search by means of discussions for the God who cannot be defined in words, He will depart further from you than He was before. If you search for Him by faith, wisdom will stand where wisdom lives, at the gates. Where wisdom is, wisdom will be seen, at least in part. But wisdom is also to some extent truly attained when the invisible God is the object of faith, in a way beyond our understanding, for we must believe in God, invisible as He is, though He is partially seen by a heart that is pure."
(Saint Columban, Abbot [540–640 AD], *Instruction 1 de Fide*, 3–5)

A Prayer to the Holy Spirit

O Holy Spirit, Beloved of my soul, I adore You,
enlighten, guide, strengthen and console me.
Tell me what I ought to say and do,
and command me to do it.

I promise to be submissive in everything You will ask of me
and to accept all that You permit to happen to me,
only show me what is Your will.

(Joseph Cardinal Mercier)

CHAPTER 1

Job's Situation
Job 1–2

Naked I came from my mother's womb, and naked shall I return;
the LORD gave, and the LORD has taken away;
blessed be the name of the LORD.
Job 1:21

The Book of Job is generally considered to be a difficult book. The book certainly has its share of difficulties with regard to textual problems and structure. It would be more accurate however, to say that the perceived difficulty arises from a difficult subject matter, namely, something that touches upon our human condition and invades our being: suffering. At the same time, this is also the reason that the book has held such a strong fascination for all kinds of readers throughout history.

The book deals with a pious, God-fearing person in profound anxiety and grief because, without informing him, God made him the object of a bet and then abandoned him in utter darkness. The coexistence of suffering, especially undeserved suffering, with the good and almighty God is the eternal problem for humanity. All religions and all philosophies have tried to find a satisfying answer. Does the Book of Job provide an answer?

In some way, it is probably best not to view Job as an answer to a theological problem, because the book is literally full of questions. A more profound reason for not considering the Book as an answer is that it is not so much about suffering as a problem to be solved, but rather, it is about God who constitutes the real mystery for humans. Who is God? Is He the kind of god that people honor in order to get some benefit in return? Such is the claim of Satan in the prologue. But God "believes" in the faith of Job and dares Satan. The friends of Job reduce God to a theory to be defended, but Job refuses such a god. Job agrees with his friends that his misery has something to do with God, but while they speak of God as a mysterious object, Job speaks to God as a person and argues with Him. Job passionately refuses to believe in a god who corresponds neatly to a man-made theological argument, and by this refusal he "saves" God and slowly begins to discover the true face of God.

There is also another way, however, in which the Book of Job could be read as a kind of biblical answer to suffering. As such it is both a devastatingly human experience and a divinely revealed mystery. As an answer the Book of Job is neither simple nor difficult. It is not simple because we are complex beings and our experiences can be complex to the point of being chaotic, yet it is not difficult because ultimately it boils down to only one thing: a personal relationship between God and us, and that is something we can never completely control. The solution of the Book is somehow simple: Job is a man of faith and in the end he finds God. It is the path leading up to this solution that is contorted and difficult: it has to do with radically giving up one's last hope and unexpectedly finding new hope.

The Shape of the Book — Modern philosophy teaches that form and content can never be completely separated. This certainly holds true for the Book of Job. The literary form in which Job is molded is deeply significant. Part of the mystery of the Book of Job resides precisely in its unique structure. There is both a surface-structure that can easily be gleaned from a quick overview and also a deep-structure that requires great attention to detail. The surface structure is as follows:

Job 1–2	Prologue (in prose)
Job 3	Job complains (monologue)
Job 4–26	Job and his three friends: Eliphaz, Bildad and Zophar; each friend makes interventions and Job answers.
	Job 4–14 First cycle, 270 verses
	Job 15–26 Second cycle 270 verses
Job 27–28	Job's first argument
Job 28	*Hymn about Wisdom*
Job 29–31	Job's second argument
Job 32-37	Intervention by a fourth friend: Elihu
Job 38–39	God's first answer
Job 40:6–41	God's second answer
Job 42:1-6	Job converts himself
Job 42:7–17	Epilogue (in prose)

The deep structure is discovered by paying close attention to subtle strophic *(verse)* arrangements and recurring words. These literary devices indicate various themes and developments. Expressions can remain the same while meanings are being developed to disclose a deeper reality.

The Prologue — In the entire Sacred Scripture there is an underlying worldview which is rarely expressed as clearly as in the framework of the Book of Job. The opening chapters of Job present the reader with the fundamental structure of reality: there is God in heaven above and there are human beings on earth below and they are connected more than even a pious man realizes. The whole structure is laid out in six well-balanced scenes:

Job 1:1-5	First prologue on earth: *Job*, a man too good to be true
Job 1:6-12	First prologue in heaven: the suspicion of *Satan*
Job 1:13-22	Four disasters come down on Job (Job 1:20–22 First answer of Job)
Job 2:1-6	Second prologue in heaven; again *Satan*
Job 2:7-10	Second prologue on earth; the wife of *Job* (Job 2:10 Second answer of Job)
Job 2:11-13	Three friends come to Job

Almost Too Good to Be True – Job in the land of Uz is a man with a strange name in a strange country. No one knows for certain what his name means, or where his country is to be found. One possible meaning of Job is "where is my father?" That meaning aligns well with Job's passionate search for God. Other possible meanings include "enemy" or "repentant." Since there is nothing specific about him, Job has a universal quality. As such, Job is well suited to put before us a universal mystery, one that not only concerns the Israelites, but all human beings: God.

In Job 1:1–5, Job is described in two ways: in his relationship to Heaven, as to God, and in his relationship to earth, to his family and his possessions. The relationship to God is clearly the most telling feature for it frames all other relationships. In Job 1:1 he is first described outwardly, as he is perceived by others, namely as a person who is blameless and upright, God-fearing and having nothing to do with evil, and then, in Job 1:5, his inner life is revealed and the reader even gets to hear that Job continually thinks of God in his innermost heart.

Being *blameless* puts Job on a par with people like Noah and Abraham (Genesis 6:9; 17:1). This means that Job is innocent and perfect in all he does. Being *upright* means that Job is law-abiding, truly just in his dealings with God and his fellow men. *God-fearing* means that he respects God and takes God into account in all he does. *Having nothing to do with evil* sums up the quality of Job, a quality that is demonstrated by his daily custom of atoning even for the hidden sins of his seven sons and three daughters. In a word, Job is a man almost too good to be true.

Retribution — Apart from his spotless behavior Job is also exceedingly wealthy, so that he was easily *the greatest of all the people of the east* (Job 1:3). He is the very icon of fidelity to God, and therefore also of happiness and wealth, for such is the understanding of retribution of the Ancient Near East: God blesses the blameless and just. The full formulation of this teaching also answers the problem of evil: God rewards the just and punishes the evildoers. Wisdom books often faithfully reflect this deeply rooted idea of retribution: *The perverse man is an abomination to the Lord, but the upright are in his confidence. The Lord's curse is on the house of the wicked, but he blesses the abode of the righteous* (Proverbs 3:32-33).

Underlying this idea of retribution is a certain worldview, in which human life is thought to be completely over at the time of death. Faith in life after death begins to develop in the third century BC. Until then, divine retribution for both good and evil can only be imagined as taking place during life on earth. The older portions of the Book of Proverbs state: *If the righteous is repaid on earth, how much more the wicked and the sinner!* (Proverbs 11:31). For the wise there is a strict coherence between what a person does and the resulting consequences. Experience seems to confirm this. *A slack hand causes poverty, but the hand of the diligent makes rich* (Proverbs 10:4). But the connection between deed and consequence is not perceived as an impersonal mechanism. God is the ultimate guarantor in this worldview. God works in such a way that His actions requite what humans do.

Job would not dream of challenging the prevailing teaching about retribution. In fact, he starts out by strongly advocating it. But, an experience will be shown to change that, for it does not really bear out this worldview. It is not that there are somewhere evildoers who have successful lives, but Job suddenly finds himself on the edge of society for no conceivable reason at all. This is what the Book of Job is about: the wise of Israel themselves started to doubt this blueprint of reality.

Suspicious, ambiguous Satan — The description of Job might seem exaggerated, but it is certainly true, since God uses the same expressions (Job 1:8) and even calls Job *my servant*, as he did with Abraham (Genesis 26:24; Psalm 105:6, 42), Moses (Numbers 12:7–8; Malachi 4:4), and David (1 Chronicles 17:4–7; Psalm 89:3, 20; Isaiah 37:35; Jeremiah 33:21–26; Ezekiel 34:23; 37:24). But at this point someone else, who in his own way also takes orders from God, enters the picture: Satan. His name means "accuser, adversary" and this is really a description of his function in the heavenly court (Psalm 82:1). Satan is counted among the *"sons of God."* This may come as a surprise to modern readers who already benefit from the knowledge of the later books of Scripture with a more complete depiction of Satan.

As the idea of retribution and the connoted idea of God undergo a slow development in the course of the biblical revelation, so also the understanding of Satan deepens. In the Book of Job and various other Old Testament books Satan is not yet seen as the devil he actually is. Job never mentions Satan in all his conversations with his friends, nor does Satan appear in the epilogue. In books of the Bible written later, God's angelic messenger comes as adversary (as Satan) to Balaam (Numbers 22:22–32). In Zechariah 3:1–2 Satan is mentioned in the same function. In books written later, Satan sheds this ambiguous role and reveals his true face of evil (1 Chronicles 21:1; Genesis 3).

The role of Satan in the prologue appears to be that of a heavenly inspector who has to make sure that humans are God-fearing for the right reasons. Satan's question, *Does Job fear God for nothing?* (Job 1:9) is crucial. It functions as a trigger. The question is not malicious per se, yet it catapults Job into unspeakable grief. At the same time, however, it provides Job (and the reader) with the only possibility to discover what it means to have nothing to lean on besides God.

It is easy enough to be devout when good behavior is rewarded, and everything is going well. But inexplicable suffering will force Job to think outside of the old box of simple retribution and discern better who God is. God has faith in Job and agrees that Job is being put to the test. In doing so God does not hide in his omniscience and respects Job's freedom, but the limit imposed on Satan makes it clear that nothing will happen outside of God's plan (see also Job 2:3). Job does not know about this deal and its stipulations, but the reader does and is therefore better enabled to understand what is coming.

Evil strikes Job, but Job does not strike back (yet) — Job remains alone. All his belongings are destroyed, stolen, or burnt in one day and all his sons and daughters perish in a natural catastrophe. Moreover, he has no idea why this has happened. His bereavement will bring to light what motivated Job in life. Job's faith turns out to be heroic. Without any external support and in great anguish he professes his faith: *Naked I came from my* *mother's womb, and naked shall I return; the Lord gave, and the Lord has taken away; blessed be the name of the Lord* (Job 1:21). As a profession of faith it is not only heroic, but also beautiful, beautifully formulated.

But precisely in its beauty lies a problem. Faith does not need to be beautiful, it needs only to be authentic. Satan is not satisfied with this beautiful profession of faith and presses for another test. God agrees to it. Job is struck with *loathsome sores from the sole of his foot to the crown of his head* (Job 2:7). This provokes Job's wife to say what Satan had in mind: *Do you still hold fast your integrity? Curse God and die* (compare Job 2:5 and 2:9). Does Satan have a point? Why did God agree to the second test after such a beautiful profession of faith? The bitter words of Job's wife really put the finger on the sore spot. What good is there in beautifully professing one's faith if reality is so ugly? Unknowingly she defends a kind of religion that is conditioned by what we see of God's actions: we only bless Him when He blesses us, and we curse Him when evil comes our way.

True to his reputation Job remains steadfast in his faith, but now less wordy: *Shall we receive good at the hand of God, and shall we not receive evil?* (Job 2:10). Soon enough, however, the conversations with his friends will demonstrate, that Job is not content to receive evil at God's hand! Then it will be his friends who pronounce beautiful, prefabricated formulas, and it is Job who will attack them.

Suffering is a part of our human existence. Suffering stems partly from our finitude, and partly from the mass of sin which has accumulated over the course of history, and continues to grow unabated today. Certainly we must do whatever we can to reduce suffering: to avoid as far as possible the suffering of the innocent; to soothe pain; to give assistance in overcoming mental suffering. These are obligations both in justice and in love, and they are included among the fundamental requirements of the Christian life and every truly human life. Great progress has been made in the battle against physical pain; yet the sufferings of the innocent and mental suffering have, if anything, increased in recent decades. Indeed we must do all we can to overcome suffering, but to banish it from the world altogether is not in our power.

This is simply because we are unable to shake off our finitude and because none of us is capable of eliminating the power of evil, of sin which, as we plainly see, is a constant source of suffering. Only God is able to do this: only a God who personally enters history by making himself man and suffering within history.

Pope Benedict XVI, *Saved in Hope* (November 30, 2007), 36.

1. Describe Job's personal character. Job 1:1–5

2. What blessings did Job receive from God? Job 1:2–3

3. Find and describe some righteous people in the Bible.

Genesis 7:1	
Genesis 15:6	
Genesis 39; 50:15–21	
Sirach 44:16	
Sirach 45:1–5	
Sirach 46:13–20	
Luke 1:5–6	
Hebrews 11:4	

4. List and describe some contemporary examples of righteous, godly people.

5. Explain some Old Testament uses of the term "son of God."

Genesis 6:2–4	
Job 1:6	
Hosea 11:1	
CCC 441	

6. What can you learn about Satan from these passages?

Job 1:6–8	
Matthew 4:1–11	
1 Peter 5:8	
Revelation 12:7–9	
CCC 391–395	
CCC 2851–2854	

* The Church gives us the Prayer to Saint Michael the Archangel for our protection against Satan. Find a copy of this prayer. Memorize it or write it out.

7. What can a Catholic who is hassled by evil spirits do?

Ephesians 6:10–17	
James 4:7	
1 Peter 5:6–10	
CCC 1671, 1673	

8. Describe the drama in Job 1:13–19.

9. How did Job respond to adversity? Job 1:20–22

10. Compare the sentiments in the following verses.

Job 1:21	
Ecclesiastes 5:15	
1 Timothy 6:6–7	

11. How does God evaluate Job? Job 2:3

12. What is Satan's next tactic against Job? Job 2:4–5

13. Explain the restraint God places upon Satan. Job 2:6

14. Describe the situation in Job 2:7–8.

15. What comfort and advice does Job's wife offer? Job 2:9

16. What comfort and advice should a spouse give to another? Proverbs 31:10–12

* When have you given good advice and comfort to your spouse or close friend?

17. How does Job respond in Job 2:10?

18. Compare Job's response with other wisdom from the Bible.

Job 2:10	
Sirach 2:3–6	
James 5:10–11	

19. Who comes to visit Job in his misfortune? Job 2:11

20. How did Job's three friends respond to his tragedy? Job 2:12–13

* How can you best minister to someone who is suffering?

CHAPTER 2

Job Complains
Job 3–21

For the thing that I fear comes upon me, and what I dread befalls me.
I am not at ease, nor am I quiet; I have no rest; but trouble comes.
Job 3:25–27

Job Curses — The first to open his mouth is Job. So far only blessings and beautiful professions of faith came from his lips, but now bitterness overflows and curses flow from his mouth. The bitterness of Job is structured in three stanzas:

Job 3:3–10	1st stanza	*Let the day perish wherein I was born, and the night…* "*A man-child is conceived*" (Job 3:3) cursing the day of birth, night of conception keyword: *darkness*, night, no light
Job 3:11–19	2nd stanza	*Why did I not die at birth?* (Job 3:11) positive description of death, netherworld keyword: *rest* (Job 3:13, 17)
Job 3:20–26	3rd stanza	*Why is light given to him who is in misery, and life to the bitter in soul, who long for death* (Job 3:20–21) Generalization: "I," "a man," "they" keyword: *rest* (Job 3:26)

Job does not curse God directly to His face as Satan expected (Job 2:5), but in cursing the day on which he was born he seems to come very close to that. His wife encourages Job to *curse God and die* (Job 2:9), and Job rightly calls her foolish, but now he curses his existence and wants to die. Job even calls on professionals, who like snake charmers are skilled in rousing up Leviathan (Job 3:8), to do the cursing for them. Job, however, is not the person who needs someone else to formulate curses for him. He has not lost his touch when it comes to finding words. *"Naked I came from my mother's womb"* (Job 1:21) was Job's first, beautiful and confident profession of faith and he blessed the Name of God. Now he curses eloquently, because no one prevented him from being born *by shutting the doors of his mother's womb* (Job 3:10). Does this mean, by implication, that he curses his Creator who gave him life? Or, is the curse too beautiful, too much like his first profession of faith?

Plea or Complaint — A theme runs through all of Job's bitter complaint: darkness, death. In the beginning God created light and separated light from darkness (Genesis 1:3–4), but now Job wants this undone and he wants to return to primordial darkness (Genesis 1:2). On the first day of creation *there was evening and there was morning* (Genesis

1:5), Job goes backward in time and first curses the day of his birth, then the night of his conception. It is a reversal of creation. From his present existence-in-darkness, Job longs for a non-existence, out of time.

This is an understandable reaction, often seen in history. Sages have recorded it: *O death, how welcome is your sentence to one who is in need and is failing in strength …to one who is contrary, and has lost his patience* (Sirach 41:2). But can psychology sufficiently explain all that Job is saying? Job wants the night of his conception to be barren and never to end: *let it hope for light, but have none* (Job 3:7–9). One positive expression stands out amidst all the gloomy expressions—hope. Does Job still have hope? An attempted suicide is often a desperate cry for help. Job's bitter complaint could be just that, and, contrary to first appearance, this may not be a monologue after all.

Formally, Job does not address his friends, but they are with him and a dialogue must always begin with one person speaking. In fact, Job's bitter words do trigger a dialogue, as the first of the friends, Eliphaz responds to Job's words (Job 4:5), and this dialogue with the three friends extends at least until Job 26. *Formally,* Job also does not address God, but in content, what Job says sounds like an echo of some prayers found in the psalms. *My God, my God, why hast thou forsaken me?* (Psalm 22:1), or *Out of the depths I cry to you, O Lord* (Psalm 130:1). Similarities with the prayer language of the Old Testament are strong. Jeremiah spoke out with the same bitterness, *Cursed be the day on which I was born* (Jeremiah 20:14–18). Also, compare Job 3:24 with Psalm 42 *My tears have been my food, day and night, while men say to me continually, "Where is your God?"* (Psalm 42:3). So, when Job twice asks "Why…?" it is not a rhetorical question and it is more than an exasperation. He wants an answer!

Satan said that God had protected Job. *Have you not put a hedge about him … and all that he has?* (Job 1:10). In a play-on-words that only the reader can appreciate, Job now says, *God has hedged [me] in* (Job 3:23). God had spoken of Job as *my servant* (Job 1:8, 2:3), and now, in a similar play on words, Job longs for the netherworld, because there *the servant is free from his master* (Job 3:19). This kind of connection between the prologue and the words of Job make it clear for the reader that God is not only mentioned, but also covertly addressed. Job knows that *light is given to him* (Job 3:20, 23) and although he does not say who gives the light, and although he does not formally address God, it is quite evident that Job thinks of God and desires an answer to his questions. Searching for an answer from God is a way to maintain the relationship.

At Rest, But Not Without God — Job speaks longingly about the netherworld. He expects to find rest there. There is an unspoken presupposition in his reasoning, namely that the netherworld lies outside the range of God's power. That is precisely the reason why he compares digging a grave with digging for *a hidden treasure* (Job 3:21), for it would remove him from God's domain. This underlying worldview is found throughout the Ancient Near East and also in the Old Testament (Isaiah 38:18; Jonah 2:5; Psalm 88:6; Ecclesiastes 4:3). The netherworld is thought to be a kind of subterranean cave where all the dead people end up in a shadowy existence without any sensation. Is this what Job really wants? What he really wants is to find rest. He does not want to be without God, but to be with God in peace. He wants God to set things right. All his talk about darkness and death is a scarcely veiled plea aimed at God to act before it is too late.

Widening the Perspective — Job started out by cursing in the *first person singular* the day of his birth and the night of his conception. In the last stanza, his bitter cry assumes the *third person singular*: "a man" (Job 3:20–23). This goes to show that the Book of Job from its very beginning must be read in the perspective of all mankind. Job is emblematic for each person who is *God-fearing* (Job 1:8; 2:3) but who experiences fear and suffering. Job is about people who suffer *without cause* (Job 2:3), and struggle with the mystery of God. With the foreknowledge of the prologue, the reader is able to understand more of the book than even the main character, Job himself, knows. The story of Job, with its various plays on words, therefore, encourages the reader to identify sympathetically with Job and to penetrate further into the mystery of his or her own life.

Unbalanced Dialogue — When Job finishes his bitter plea, the friends begin to speak, one after the other, and each time Job answers them. The interventions by the friends together with Job's replies appear to be organized in cycles. Two cycles are clearly distinguishable, but the third cycle seems incomplete:

		Monologue by Job	Job 3	26 verses
1st cycle	A)	Eliphaz	Job 4–5	48 verses
		Job	Job 6–7	51 verses
	B)	Bildad	Job 8	22 verses
		Job	Job 9–10	57 verses
	C)	Zophar	Job 11	20 verses
		Job	Job 12–14	75 verses
2nd cycle	A')	Eliphaz	Job 15	35 verses
		Job	Job 16–17	38 verses
	B')	Bildad	Job 18	21 verses
		Job	Job 19	29 verses
	C')	Zophar	Job 20	29 verses
		Job	Job 21	34 verses
3rd cycle	A")	Eliphaz	Job 22	30 verses
		Job	Job 23–24	42 verses
	B")	Bildad	Job 25	6 verses
		Job	Job 26–27	37 verses
		Monologue by Job	Job 28	28 verses
		Monologue by Job	Job 29-31	91 verses*

* Number of verses as found in the RSVCE, irrespective of opening verses.

The seemingly broken third cycle clearly reveals an incongruity that is present throughout the dialogue. The dialogue is lopsided from the beginning. The answers of Job are always longer, sometimes much longer, than the corresponding interventions of the friends. Each cycle starts out more or less balanced in terms of length, but the friends have less and less to say while Job relentlessly keeps on arguing. There are two reasons for Job's persistence. First, Job's answer is always more than just a reply to what has been said by his friend. After an initial reply to the friend who intervened, there is a shift in focus and Job continues to speak directing his words toward God whom he considers to be his real opponent. Since there is no reply from God, Job's words directed to God slowly grow shorter and shorter. Job continues all alone by himself, just as he began, with a monologue. Second, there can be no argument with a man who suffers *without cause* (Job 2:3). Any such argument is bound to fail. The friends seem to realize this and say less and less, until the dialogue grinds to a complete stop.

Eliphaz — Eliphaz is inflexible. He wants Job to see it his way. Rhetorical questions are, in fact, a way to make statements that are supposedly beyond all argumentation. Eliphaz does not discuss or pose any questions at all. He is absolutely sure of his teaching. *This we have searched out; it is true* (Job 5:27).

A series of rhetorical questions are posed to prove that Job's suffering must be a just result of Job's sin. Eliphaz says *As for me, I would seek God, and to God would I commit my cause* (Job 5:8). Job *had* prayed to God, but Eliphaz didn't hear Job's prayer. While Job has prayed to God, Eliphaz gives no evidence in the text of praying to God for Job or for himself. According to Eliphaz, man is impure by nature and man is incapable of understanding his life. He has a negative view of man. *Can mortal man be righteous before God?* (Job 4:17).

Eliphaz offers traditional wisdom based on experience with the natural order. For the careful reader, the discourse is fraught with irony. *The beasts of the field shall be at peace with you* (Job 5:23), as it was in paradise. The fate of the fool is beautifully expressed. Affliction does not come from dust (Job 5:6), but man is formed out of dust (Genesis 2:7). And trouble sprouts not from the ground, but man is born to trouble, or begets trouble. By now, the reader should be wary of such beautiful phrases.

God is the guarantor of the order in the world. The clever are disappointed but there is hope for the weak. What hope does Job have? God educates man through suffering and this truth is worthy of a beatitude: *Happy is the man whom God reproves* (Job 5:17). It turns out to be literally true for Job (Job 42:12–17). Indeed, God does have a plan, but it does not happen at all in the way Eliphaz predicts. Do either Eliphaz or Job know God sufficiently? Do we?

Job gives an immediate reply. In spite of the veiled threats and unintentional irony that the reader could detect, the words of Eliphaz sounded reasonable and amicable, but on Job all reason and pretended friendship are lost, for in his suffering there is no reason

(Job 2:3), nor does he receive comfort from his friends. The answer to his friends is divided in three stanzas:

1st stanza	Job 6:2–13	Job is in a hopeless situation
2nd stanza	Job 6:14–23	He does not expect unreliability from his friends.
3rd stanza	Job 6:24–30	Job *does* expect reliable instruction from friends.

A beautiful lament — Calamity sums up Job's reality (Job 6:2–30). His situation is hopeless and his friends are insensitive and uncomprehending. Pain outweighs all reason. Job first concentrates on what has happened to him (Job 6:2–7) and then describes what he sees as the only possible way out—death (Job 6:8–13).

The poetry is sophisticated. The lament can be divided into four parts; the first and third (Job 6:2–4, 8–10) are a complaint about what God is not doing to Job; the second and fourth (Job 6:5, 7, 11–13) describe how Job deals with God's actions. The rhetorical questions are inspired by the animal kingdom in true wisdom style.

The beauty of Job's lament gives him away. He is desperate, yes. But, in his desperation he clings to a scheme of his own. Job has a hidden hope. When Job literally says *O that God would grant my desire* (Job 6:8b), he seems to long for death in order to be free from his calamities. But, having spurned the loathsome words of Eliphaz, Job emphatically confirms, while pleading to be cut off from life: *I have not denied the words of the Holy One* (Job 6:10). His death wish is not what it seems to be. He is not at all indifferent to justice. In fact, his real desire is for justice and life — on his own terms!

Classical biblical images compar[e] the productive cavity of the mother to the "depths of the earth" … there is the symbol of the potter and of the sculptor who "fashions" and molds his artistic creation, his masterpiece, just as it is said about the creation of man… Then there is a "textile" symbol that evokes the delicacy of the skin, the flesh, the nerves, "threaded" onto the bony skeleton. *Job also recalled forcefully these and other images to exalt that masterpiece which the human being is, despite being battered and bruised by suffering:* "Your hands have formed me and fashioned me … Remember that you fashioned me from clay … Did you not pour me out as milk and thicken me like cheese? With skin and flesh you clothed me, with bones and sinews knit me together" (Job 10:8–11).

The idea … that God already sees the entire future of that embryo, still an "unformed substance," is extremely powerful. The days, which that creature will live and fill with deeds, throughout his earthly existence, are already written in the Lord's Book of life. Thus, once again the transcendent greatness of divine knowledge emerges, embracing not only humanity's past and present but also the span still hidden, of the future. The greatness of this little unborn human creature, formed by God's hands and surrounded by his love appears: a biblical tribute to the human being from the first moment of his existence.

Pope Benedict XVI, *General Audience*, December 28, 2005.

1. Describe Job's emotional state in Job 3.

2. What does Job wish for? Job 3:11–16

3. Who else in the Bible shares Job's sentiments? Jeremiah 20:14–18

*Has there ever been a time in your life that you were so depressed, overwhelmed or discouraged, that you felt like Job? Explain that time.

4. Eliphaz gives a long discourse in Job 4–5. Find a summary of his argument.

Job 4:7–8	
Job 4:17	

* While Eliphaz is incorrect in assuming that suffering is *always* a result of sin, can you think of situations in which suffering *is* a result of sin?

5. What does Eliphaz recommend to Job? Job 5:8

6. Compare the following verses.

Job 5:17–18	
Hosea 6:1	
Psalm 94:10–11	
Hebrews 12:5–8	

* Share a situation in which you experienced discipline from the Lord.

7. What does Job hope to receive from his friends? Job 6:13–14

8. Explain an Old Testament understanding of death.

Job 7:6–9	
2 Samuel 12:23; 14:14	
Wisdom 2:1	

9. What can you learn about death from the New Testament?

John 14:1–3	
1 Corinthians 15:51–57	

10. How does Bildad describe God? Job 8:3–4, 20–22

11. What does Bildad suggest to Job? Job 8:5–6

12. Summarize Job's response in Job 9–10.

13. What is the theme of Zophar's speech? Job 11

14. Compare the following verses.

Job 12:14	
Revelation 3:7	

15. Describe Job's reasoning in Job 12–14.

16. What can you learn from these verses?

Job 15:8	
Wisdom 9:13	
Romans 11:33–34	
1 Corinthians 2:11–16	

17. For what does Job pray in Job 16–17?

18. Of what does Bildad accuse Job? Job 18

19. Write Job's prayer of faith and hope. Job 19:25–27

20. Contrast the thoughts of Zophar and Job from Job 20–21.

Zophar	Job 20	
Job	Job 21	

* Write your own prayer of faith and hope in God to pray during hard times.

Chapter 3

Faith and Friends
Job 22–37

For I know that my Redeemer lives,
and at last he will stand upon the earth;
and after my skin has been thus destroyed,
then from my flesh I shall see God,
whom I shall see on my side,
and my eyes shall behold, and not another.
My heart faints within me!
Job 19:25–27

A Good Man is Afflicted — Job is a righteous man in anguish. At this point in salvation history, God has not yet revealed to man the concepts of heaven, hell, and purgatory. In the Orient of Job's time, people believed that God rewarded people for their good deeds in *this* life and God punished people for their sins in *this* life as well. They had no understanding of everlasting life. People of Job's time imagined that there was a place of the dead, a type of subterranean cave that the dead would inhabit. Job's suffering is so great, that he ends up longing to go to that place. Job cannot understand what he has done to offend God and warrant such pain.

Job's friends appear to be true friends, not just "fair weather friends." When they learn of Job's misfortune, they come to comfort him. His friends sit with Job in silence for seven days and seven nights, without saying a word (Job 2:13). Job has nothing left to give them. He has been stripped of his riches and his wealth. But, he still has his faith in God and he still has his friends. They come to comfort him with their presence. Perhaps the seven days and seven nights of silence were a great comfort to Job. It can often be a ministry to simply sit with those who suffer.

Yet, Job's friends cannot hold their tongues forever. They try to help Job to discover how he has offended God, to uncover his sin, so that he can repent and get right with God. Each of Job's friends begins with the common understanding, prevalent at that time, that all suffering is the direct result of unrepentant sin. While some suffering *is* a concrete result of a specific sin (sexually promiscuous people often contract sexually transmitted diseases, drug users sometimes get infected from dirty needles, thieves end up in jail). However, innocent people might also suffer (an innocent baby can contract a disease from the mother, children sometimes get brain cancer, diabetes, or arthritis—bad things sometimes happen to good people). This concept of the innocent suffering was unknown then. God is just. Job and his friends believe that God punishes and rewards each man for his deeds in this life. Wickedness warrants retribution from God now. So, if Job is suffering, he must have committed some serious sin, or offended God in some way. After all these speeches, Job continually affirms his innocence and insists that he is righteous before God. How can Job repent for something he has not done? To confess to an imaginary sin would be dishonest, a lie. Job is confused and distraught.

Throughout the Book of Job, the reader is aware of events of which Job and his friends are unaware. The dialogue in heaven between God and Satan is revealed to the readers of the Bible, but not to Job and his wife and friends. There is no way for Job and his friends to discover the theological treatment of suffering that the readers of the Book of Job can ponder. The Holy Spirit inspires the human author of the Book of Job to teach something to seekers for all time. The suffering of the innocent perplexed the people in ancient times and making sense out of suffering remains a mysterious challenge to people in contemporary times as well.

The Servant of the Lord — Job continues to demonstrate that he is a man of faith. While Job listens to the accusations of his friends, he creates longer and longer rebuttals. Job not only speaks to his friends, but also cries out to God. Is God Job's friend? Has He abandoned Job? Does God care that Job is suffering and in pain?

Job's friends are unaware of God's evaluation of Job. But, the reader of the Bible learns that God said to Satan: *"Have you considered my servant Job, that there is none like him on the earth, a blameless and upright man, who fears God and turns away from evil?"* (Job 1:8). To be called "the servant of the Lord" was the highest praise for a man in the Old Testament. Abraham, Moses, and David were called "servant of the Lord." In Numbers, God says, *"...If there is a prophet among you, I the Lord make myself known to him in a vision, I speak with him in a dream. Not so with my servant Moses; he is entrusted with all my house. With him I speak mouth to mouth, clearly, and not in dark speech; and he beholds the form of the Lord"* (Numbers 12:6–8). Similarly, Solomon recalls that his father David was the servant of the Lord. *O God of Israel, let your word be confirmed, which you have spoken to your servant David my father* (1 Kings 8:26).

Through his pain and suffering, Job insists on his innocence. He has been faithful to God. He has maintained his integrity and tried to live an upright and blameless life. What has he done to warrant such adversity? Job somehow clings to his faith in God. While hope wanes in Job, he clings to his own scheme, but that does not work. So he hopes that someone in the heavenly court will speak on his behalf. Little does he know that the opposite is the case, but the reader knows.

The Christian perspective of Job's prayer in Job 19:25–27 is entirely different. Job has not reached that point of faith where he surrenders completely to God. That will only come in Job 42:1–7. *Redeemer* normally is a close relative (Ruth 4), which is not the case here for Job knows that they are all against him (Job 19:13–22). Here it probably refers to the impartial heavenly referee (Job 9:33) or the heavenly witness (Job 13:19). Job hopes that at least someone will *stand up* for him, which is a term that refers to a juridical defense.

Each of Job's friends gives impassioned speeches to try to get Job to repent to God, say his prayers, and shape up. They begin gently, but become increasingly harsh and accusatory. God is good and just. The fate of the wicked is suffering. Clearly, Job has done something to deserve his punishment. However, Job doesn't have a clue concerning what he has done to offend God. Job has been faithful to God, but God remains distant and mysterious. Job experiences the tension between his perceived obedience to God, and God's freedom to remain distant, which human minds cannot fathom.

People of all times observe that sometimes the righteous are not rewarded in this life, and sometimes the wicked are not punished. Job presents the plight of the poor and needy in Chapter 24. *From out of the city the dying groan, and the soul of the wounded cries for help; yet God pays no attention to their prayer* (Job 24:12). God doesn't always answer the prayer of the suffering in the way that one hopes.

Furthermore, Job makes a striking contrast between light and darkness: *"There are those who rebel against the light, who are not acquainted with its way, and do not stay in its paths. The murderer rises in the dark, that he may kill the poor and needy; and in the night he is as a thief. The eye of the adulterer also waits for the twilight, saying, 'No eye will see me'; and he disguises his face"* (Job 24:13–15). Job observes that sometimes, it seems that the wicked do get away with murder. Evil deeds go unpunished in this life. Is God uncaring? Doesn't God see?

According to Jeremiah 18:18, three sources of guidance were available to people in ancient times: (1) the law of the priest, (2) the counsel of the wise, and (3) the word of the prophet. A reflection on wisdom appears in Job 28. *"But where shall wisdom be found? And where is the place of understanding? Man does not know the way to it, and it is not found in the land of the living ... God understands the way to it, and he knows its place ... 'Behold the fear of the Lord, that is wisdom; and to depart from evil is understanding'"* (Job 28:12–13, 23, 28). An important truth emerges here. God's ways are above man's understanding. Suffering is a mystery that may not be fully understood in this life. But, there is hope for understanding in the life to come, for those who trust in God and hope in Him.

Honor has turned to shame. Job experiences a dark night of the soul. God seems very far from him. Job recalls his previous happiness, when God was with him, blessing him. Job was a father to the poor and enjoyed the adulation of many. People would come to him for wise counsel and heed his words. But his prior honor has now turned to shame. Men mock Job and make sport of him. People abhor him and keep aloof from him because God has humbled him. Job concludes his reflections by again asserting his integrity. Job asks to be weighed in a balance. He lists common sins and pleads "not guilty" to each of them in Job 31. This is the classical oath formula and Job's last attempt at drawing God out. If God does not do any of those bad things, it proves that Job is innocent. So Job basically turns the "no response" from God into a kind of response that supports his own viewpoint. Job has not yet surrendered to God.

Suddenly, seemingly out of the blue, a brash young man, named Elihu, whose name means "He is my God," comes to address Job and his peers. It seems as if Elihu has been listening to the speeches and finds fault with the dialogue. Elihu appears to be angry because he believes that they have not spoken well and he believes that he has more wisdom than his elders and can explain their dilemma to them. Elihu doesn't really say anything much that is new or particularly wise, but he speaks with the zeal and self-confidence of a prophet who knows how God sees the situation.

Elihu begins by saying that wisdom does not always come with age. Youth can also possess wisdom as a gift from God. Interestingly, unlike the three friends, Elihu addresses Job by name (Job 33:1). He reiterates the same arguments that have been advanced previously. God is greater than man. Perhaps God has spoken to Job in a dream or a nightmare, but Job is not listening. Job and all of the friends have proclaimed the justice of God. Elihu restates the obvious with greater passion, the passion of a prophet who can be ignored or accepted, but with whom one cannot argue: *"For according to the work of a man he will repay him, and according to his ways he will make it befall him. Of a truth, God will not do wickedly, and the Almighty will not pervert justice"* (Job 34:11–12).

Elihu's understanding is not sophisticated, but has an insistence and a hammering quality which drives the point home. As a result, Job remains silent, which is amazing He who could not stop talking, now remains silent for six chapters. There is much to ponder. It may not be the direct voice of God, which he longed to hear, but he cannot ignore a messenger with such a God-like name. Job in his wisdom realizes that some times bad things happen to good people. Sometimes, the innocent suffer. It can be a mystery to try to make sense out of suffering. Elihu states: *"He [God] does not keep the wicked alive, but gives the afflicted their right"* (Job 36:6). But, wait a minute. Is this true? Does God wipe out the wicked, or does He allow them to live? Does God always immediately help the afflicted?

Wisdom speaks from experience. Youth lack experience, and tend to see things as black or white. Job has lived long enough to know that sometimes the wicked prosper. And often the poor and the needy suffer in their affliction. Job expected his friends to show him compassion, kindness, loyalty, and faithfulness. He expected that his friends would believe in his innocence. But, Job received harshness and criticism from his friends. If only he would acknowledge his sin, shape up, and repent before God, then surely God would alleviate his suffering. Indeed, God will alleviate Job's suffering. God does not demand false humility or hypocritical repentance, but Job cannot put his own terms onto God.

> The task to which the Lord calls you is the "apostolate of friendship." Every Christian is asked to be a friend of God and with God's grace, attracts his own friends to Him.
> Pope Benedict XVI, *Audience*, April 10, 2006

1. Summarize Eliphaz's argument from these passages.

Job 22:21–29	
Matthew 23:12	
Luke 1:50–54	

2. How has Job responded to God's commands?

Job 23:11–12	
Psalm 119:10–11	
Psalm 119:97–107	

3. Find the imagery concerning darkness.

Job 24:13–14	
Job 24:15	
Job 24:16–17	
John 3:19–21	

* Has there been a time in your life when you came out of darkness into the light? Or, has there been a time when the "lights turned on" for you and you saw God's goodness, mercy and love? Please explain that time.

4. What can you learn from these verses?

Job 26:6	
Psalm 139:7–12	

* Have you ever tried to "hide" from God?

5. What theological virtue is posed in the following verses?

Job 11:18	
Job 19:10	
Job 27:6	
Proverbs 10:28	
Romans 8:24	
CCC 1817	

6. Define wisdom and give an example. CCC 1831

* Describe a person you know who has the spiritual gift of wisdom.

7. Where shall wisdom be found?

Job 28:12–28	
Ecclesiastes 7:23–24	
Wisdom 7:7–11	
Baruch 3:1	
Romans 11:33–36	
Colossians 2:2–3	

8. Where does wisdom come from? Sirach 1:1

9. How does Job reminisce about his early days? Job 29:1–20

10. What was Job's previous stature among his kinsmen? Job 29:21–25

* Have you ever experienced a reversal of fortune?

11. How do people react to Job in his current adversity? Job 30:1–15

12. What kind of a friend was Job to others? Job 30:25

13. What does Job expect and receive from his friends?

Job 6:14–15	
Job 30:26	
Sirach 6:14–17	
Sirach 6:8	

* Describe someone who has been a faithful friend to you in hard times.

14. Find some prayers of lamentation and examples of lamentation.

Job 30:27–31	
Lamentation 1:20–21	
Micah 2:4	
Matthew 2:18	

15. Describe Elihu. Job 32

16. How many times can you find Elihu described as "angry?" Job 32:1–5

17. Later, how does Elihu speak of this emotion? Job 36:13

18. How does Elihu think God is speaking to Job? Job 33:14–17

19. What truism is repeated in Job 34:11 and Job 36:6–7, 11?

20. How should a true friend behave?

Job 19:21	
Proverbs 18:24	
Sirach 22:22–25	
John 15:14–17	

Monthly Social Activity

This month, your small group will meet for coffee, tea, or a simple breakfast, lunch, or dessert in someone's home. Pray for this social event and for the host or hostess. Try, if at all possible, to attend.

After a short prayer and some time for small talk, write a few sentences about a "time when you felt like Job," or a time when you acted like Job's friends. If time permits, share about someone who has been a true friend in times of adversity. Make sure that everyone has time to share.

Examples

◆ *Shortly after experiencing a death in the family, we also experienced unemployment. No matter how hard we tried and prayed, the situation just seemed to get worse.*

◆ *When my friend experienced a series of hardships, I just kept saying that "it must be God's will." I don't think that my sentiments brought much comfort or help.*

◆ *Even though many things seemed to go wrong when I was younger, my brother stood by me, offering comfort and encouragement. God seemed to bring good out of the adversity. Now, I can see that God had a plan all along.*

CHAPTER 4

God Answers
Job 38–42

I had heard of you by the hearing of the ear,
but now my eye sees you;
therefore, I despise myself,
and repent in dust and ashes.
Job 42:5–6

The Lord answers Job — God was speaking in heaven at the beginning of the Book of Job, but has remained silent since Chapter 2. For the friends of Job, it was unnecessary for God to answer Job, because the problem was clear to them. Job had sinned and God had justly punished him. There was a simple cause and effect relationship. Those who obey God are rewarded in this life. Those who sin against God are punished with suffering in this world.

Throughout the book, Job has been pressuring God to answer him. He seems to be saying, "Hurry up, I'm dying. Rescue me." Job's hope begins to wane. Finally, Job loses complete hope in his own righteousness. And when he loses hope in himself, then he is free to accept a new hope, a hope based on who God is—a good and just God. Job's greatest pain comes from his confusion about his relationship with God. In Job 29, Job recalls when he and God were friends. But in Job 13:24, Job imagines himself as God's enemy. Job must lose hope in his own righteousness. Then his soul becomes fertile ground for God to place the theological virtue of hope in him. Job must be born again. He must be reborn into a new hope.

When the energetic Elihu finishes his message, he has brought Job to silence and reflection. For so long, Job had pressured God to answer him. He wanted a trial before God. But, now Job is silent, realizing better than before that God is the judge. God does not pronounce His verdict in the way Job expects. Rather, God questions Job! A series of rhetorical questions highlight the magnificence and majesty of God's creation. Who can fully understand God's creation? The interplay of light and darkness, birth and death unfold in Job 38:12–21. Who can understand the patterns of weather: snow, rain, ice, lightning, and clouds (Job 38:22–38)?

And, what about the animal kingdom? God presents five pairs of wild animals: (1) the lion and raven (Job 38:39–41), (2) the mountain goat and hind (Job 39:1–4), (3) the wild donkey and wild ox (Job 39:9–12), (4) the ostrich and the horse (Job 39:13–25), and (5) the hawk and eagle (Job 39:26–30). Ancient art presented these animals associated with evil, darkness, and chaos. Yet God controls these animals and protects humans from them. The point is obvious: God is in charge of the whole universe.

Job answers God — Now God presses Job to answer (Job 40:2), and Job answers with resignation. Previously Job had recalled how he was held in honor and esteem by his fellow man (Job 29). But now Job recognizes that compared with the Almighty, he is of small account. Job wanted God to respond to him on Job's terms. But like every human being on the planet, Job must learn to accept God on God's terms for who God is, not who man imagines God to be. Job is silent before God. He does not confess any sin. For God will not accept a lie, no matter how humble or well intended. Job is caught up into the mystery of God and His ways.

God continues His dialogue with Job and turns the tables. He puts Job in the judgment seat. *"Will you even put me in the wrong? Will you condemn me that you may be justified? Have you an arm like God, and can you thunder with a voice like his?"* (Job 40:8–9). Must Job point a finger to condemn God in order to assert his innocence? Is Job big enough to contend with God? Can man deal with wickedness better than God can, with greater justice?

Evil exists in this world. God describes two monsters. Behemoth, a strong land beast (Job 40:15–24), has bones like bronze and limbs like iron. Leviathan (Job 41:1–34) a sea monster, cannot be subdued by the mightiest men. God does not destroy these beasts, but He limits their power. These beasts may be analogous to man's free will. Man is free to strut about and boast and cause trouble. God does not wipe out all wickedness immediately, but may allow it for a time. Ultimately though, God has a plan. God is the master of the universe, and does not let it fall into chaos. God shows continuing providence for all of His creation.

Finally, in the very last chapter of the book, Job is truly humbled and repents. He does not repent in terms of a confession of sin, which would be a lie. Rather, Job repents in terms of "changing his mind" about his inadequate understanding of God and His justice. Job has been on a journey of faith.

Initially, Job thought that God was his friend. Job was described as an upright and blameless man, almost too good to be true. Certainly Job was better than most of us are. So, if a blameless man cannot get to God on his own terms, neither can a sinful man manipulate God to do his bidding. No one in the universe can come to God by his own merits. Man is not in control. God is the one in control. We are creatures. God is the Creator. God's wisdom knows all things. We see dimly (1 Corinthians 13:12).

"I know that you can do all things" **(Job 42:2).** Job acknowledges the power of God. God is Almighty and can do all things. Others in the pages of the Bible will make the same discovery and find God in impossible situations. The Angel Gabriel will tell the Virgin Mary *"For with God nothing will be impossible"* (Luke 1:37). And later, after Jesus cures a blind man, an impossible feat, Peter proclaims: *"You are the Christ"* (Mark 8:29). Then Jesus announces, *that the Son of man must suffer many thing* (Mark 8:31). Jesus will suffer greater things than Job suffered. Still later, Jesus tells a man with a sick child, *"All things are possible to him who believes"* (Mark 9:23). Recognizing that God can do all things acknowledges that God is in control. Job acknowledges his position before God. God is the source of all wisdom, power, and justice. Human beings have limited understanding.

"I had heard of you by the hearing of the ear; but now my eye sees you;" (Job 42:5). Job had heard of God as all humans do. The majesty of God is manifest in the wonders of the universe and beauty of creation (Romans 1:19–20). Job sought God sincerely and tried to live in a way pleasing to God. But, now Job comes to know God in a deeply personal way. Job demonstrates the difference between "knowing about God," and "knowing God." God reveals Himself to those who seek Him with a pure heart in humility and prayer. Every seeker and every believer waits in humble, eager anticipation for God to reveal more of Himself in love.

The story of Job was framed with a narrative prologue at the beginning and another narrative epilogue at the end. In the end, Job finds what he was seeking from God. He learns that God is his friend. God has not abandoned him in his suffering. But, God was there, the silent friend, listening to him all along.

In the end, Job, the friends of Job, and the readers of the Bible learn that Job's suffering was not the result of sin. Suffering remains a mystery. Sometimes suffering may be the result of sin. Some suffering may be God's way of testing the righteous or proving the steadfastness of one's faith. Or suffering may be God's means of disciplining, training, or strengthening a believer. While we may never understand the suffering of the innocent, we can hope in God's mercy and trust in His divine justice. We should refrain from judging friends too quickly and too harshly. God's wisdom and knowledge far surpass human understanding.

God exonerates Job. At the beginning of the book, Satan had predicted that Job would blaspheme God. Satan was proved wrong. In all his suffering and adversity, Job did not curse God. Now, God indicates that Job has spoken rightly of God (Job 42:7). How did Job do this? What can you learn from this? Job spoke in a proper way. He told the truth. He examined his conscience correctly, and he appeared to have a very well developed conscience. Job cried out to God. He argued. He lamented. Often in the Bible, a prayer of lamentation ends in praise of God (Psalm 22, Psalm 28). Jesus lamented to His Father during His agony in the garden and in His Crucifixion. In Job's brokenness, he cries out for a friend, a mediator, a vindicator. Only after Job reaches the bottom of his barrel, and says, "I'm finished," does God come to the rescue. God is Job's friend and Job is God's friend. They have been friends all along, even through the hard times.

Similarly, in the human condition, when a person realizes his brokenness, his neediness, his insufficiency, then he can turn to God for mercy and redemption. Self-righteousness may try to mask the inherent truth that each person needs a Savior, a Redeemer. Only after acknowledging one's total dependence upon God can healing and restoration begin. Self-sufficiency is a ruse. God is too big, and our relationship with God too deep to be contained in intellectual suppositions. At the center of the mystery and in the midst of the suffering and pain, Job respected the freedom of God. And God in His freedom chose to reveal Himself personally to Job and his friends.

Suffering is a major theme in the Book of Job and so is friendship. What is true friendship? Who is a faithful friend? Job's friends came from afar to comfort him. They sat with him in silence for seven days and seven nights (Job 2:13). But, when Job began to lament and pray to God the friends immediately entered into the debate. They defend God against Job. However, do they really defend God, or do they defend their small and inadequate understanding of God? Job's friends never prayed to God on his behalf. They only accuse and debate with him.

Where is an example of faithful friendship to be found? Job stood by his children, offering sacrifices to God on their behalf, in case they had committed any inadvertent sin (Job 1:5). Job had been a true friend to the poor, the fatherless, and the widow (Job 29:12–13). Job gave counsel to those who had no confidence (Job 29:21–24). Job wept for those who suffered hardships (Job 30:25). Job was a faithful friend, listening, counseling, helping, and comforting those in need.

In the end, Job proves to be a faithful friend to Eliphaz, Bildad, Zophar, and Elihu, too. God tells the friends of Job to offer sacrifice and ask Job to pray for them, that God will not deal with them according to their folly (Job 42:8). Earlier, Zophar told Job that if he confessed his sin, he would once again prosper and people would come asking his intercession (Job 11:13–19). Zophar's prophecy is fulfilled in the end, and it is Zophar who must ask for Job's intercession (Job 42:9). Good friend that Job was, he prayed for them and averted their deserved punishment.

Job's story began with blessings and prosperity. He lost everything, except his faith and his friends. After Job suffered for a time, God restored his hope, and gave Job a deeper faith. He restored all his fortunes. And, the greatest blessing of all was the restoration of Job's relationship with God. God gave Job the theological virtues of faith, hope, and love, without which all life is meaningless and futile and leads only to despair. Friendship with God allows man to suffer in hope, anticipating the joy of heaven at the end of human suffering.

God is the foundation of hope: not any god, but the God who has a human face and who has loved us to the end, each one of us, and humanity in its entirety.

Prayer as a school of hope — A first essential setting for learning hope is prayer. When no one listens to me any more, God still listens to me. When I can no longer talk to anyone or call upon anyone, I can always talk to God. When there is no longer anyone to help me deal with a need or expectation that goes beyond the human capacity for hope, he can help me.

Pope Benedict XVI, *Saved In Hope* (November 30, 2007), 31–32.

1. How does God begin to address Job? Job 38:1–4

2. Identify some poetic imagery from nature in Job 38:8–11.

3. Find references to death and length of life in Job 38:17–21.

4. Pick out some phrases about nature and weather in Job 38:22–38.

5. List some pairs of wild animals found in creation.

Job 38:39–41	
Job 39:1–2	
Job 39:13–25	
Job 39:26–30	

6. What challenge does God present to Job? Job 40:1–2

7. How does Job respond to God? Job 40:3–5

8. What virtue is necessary to approach God? CCC 2559

* List some practical ways in which you could grow in the virtue of humility.

9. How does God respond to Job's challenges? Job 40:6–14

10. Describe Behemoth. Job 40:15–24

11. What can you learn about Leviathan? Job 41

12. Compare the following statements.

Job 40:2; 42:2	
Luke 1:37	
Matthew 19:26	
Mark 10:27	
CCC 275	

* Have you ever seen God work in a seemingly impossible situation for you?

13. What does Job confess in Job 42:3?

14. How and why did God create the world and for what purpose? CCC 299

15. What virtues did Job need?

Job 11:18	
Romans 8:24–25	

16. Explain the difference between "knowing about God" and "knowing God."

Romans 1:19–20	
Job 19:25–27	
Job 42:5	

* Brainstorm practical ways in which you could come to know God better.

17. What did God say to Job's friends? Job 42:7–8

18. Find a prophecy of Zophar that was fulfilled.

Job 11:19b	
Job 42:8–9	

19. What happened to Job's wealth? Job 42:10–12

20. Tell the happy ending of Job's story. Job 42:13–17

CHAPTER 5

Psalms Book I
Psalms 1–41

Blessed is the man
who walks not in the counsel of the wicked,
nor stands in the way of sinners,
nor sits in the seat of scoffers;
but his delight is in the law of the LORD,
and on his law he meditates day and night.
He is like a tree planted by streams of water,
that yields its fruit in its season,
and its leaf does not wither.
In all that he does, he prospers.
The wicked are not so,
but are like chaff which the wind drives away.
Therefore the wicked will not stand in the judgment,
nor sinners in the congregation of the righteous;
for the LORD knows the way of the righteous,
but the way of the wicked will perish.
Psalm 1:1–6

Some of the most beautiful poetry in the Wisdom literature of the Bible can be found in the Book of Psalms—the Psalter. In Hebrew, this book is entitled *Tehillim*, meaning "Prayers of Praise." At the heart of each of the one hundred fifty psalms is the Lord, the Holy One of Israel, Almighty God. Each individual psalm speaks directly to God or praises His glory and grandeur in speaking about Him.

Psalms retain their beauty and mystery over thousands of years. Even to this day, compact disc recordings of monks and nuns singing the Gregorian chant of the psalms in Latin appeal to believers as well as seekers. The psalms provide the basic framework for the Divine Office or Liturgy of the Hours, prayed by priests and religious throughout the world, as well as by prayerful lay men and women. In each Mass, the first reading is always followed by a psalm. Ideally the psalm should be sung or chanted. Saint Jerome revealed that in his day prayerful women studied the Hebrew language in order to better understand and to pray the psalms.

Reading the psalms turns one's heart to prayer. The psalms are intended for singing. And after hearing a particular psalm sung beautifully and piercingly at Mass, the melody remains in the heart and mind. The psalms are so powerful and so moving that the Synod of Laodicea (AD 360) ruled that only psalms were to be sung during the official liturgy. Today, different composers have set many psalms to music with more than one melody. So, there are many melodies to accompany Psalm 23, for example.

> A psalm is the prayer of praise of the people of God, the exaltation of the Lord, the joyful song of the congregation, the cry of all humanity, the applause of the universe, the voice of the Church, the sweet-sounding confession of faith, ... blessed freedom, a cry of happiness, an echo of joy. A psalm softens wrath, relieves care, and lightens sorrow. It is a weapon at night, teaching in the day, a shield in fear, a festival celebration in holiness, an image of quietness, the pledge of peace and harmony. The psalm arises at day's beginning and is still sounding at day's end.
>
> Saint Ambrose (AD 340–397), *Commentary on Psalm 1*, 64.7

The Psalter is actually a compendium of 150 separate and distinct prayer poems or hymns, inspired by the Holy Spirit and composed by different human authors. Seventy-three of the psalms, distributed throughout the book, are ascribed to David, twelve to Asaph, eleven to the sons of Korah, two to Solomon (Psalms 72 and 126), one to Heman (Psalm 88), one to Ethan (Psalms 89), and one to Moses (Psalm 90). In antiquity, psalms were learned by heart and sung collectively.

Psalm headings or superscriptions indicate technical musical instructions for performance, the type of instrument preferred, the name of the author, and sometimes the historical references. Psalms 3 and 4 include all of these components. "A Psalm of David, when he fled from Absalom his son" introduces Psalm 3. And, Psalm 4 begins, "To the choirmaster: with stringed instruments." Some of the headings include technical musical terms, while the meaning of other terms, such as *miktam, maskil,* and *siggayon,* are unclear to us. *Mizmor* means "hymns" or "psalms"; *shir* means "song"; *lelammed* "teaching"; *tefillah* "prayer"; and *shiggaion* "lament."

Greek translations resulted in different numbering from the Hebrew psalms. The Greek and Latin translations probably correctly combined Psalms 9 and 10, and combined Psalms 114 and 115 into a single psalm, while dividing Psalm 116 in two. The respective numbering of the Psalms results roughly in the following.

Hebrew *New American, Jerusalem, RSVCE*	Greek–Latin *Douay-Rheims*
Psalms 1–8	Psalms 1–8
Psalms 9–10	Psalm 9
Psalms 11–113	Psalms 10–112
Psalms 114–115	Psalm 113
Psalms 116	Psalms 114–115
Psalms 117–146	Psalms 116–145
Psalm 147	Psalms 146–147
Psalms 148–150	Psalms 148–150

The Book of Psalms falls within a beautiful frame. Psalms 1 and 2 provide a programmatic preface to the psalter with the final "Hallel" Psalms 146–150 closing the Psalter in a hymn of praise to God's goodness. The division of the Psalter into five books may have been analogous to the Pentateuch, the five books of Moses. An early *midrash* (commentary on the Hebrew scriptures) proclaimed: "As Moses gave the five books of the *torah* to the Israelites, so David gave them the five books of Psalms." Each of the books ends in a concluding doxology, a verse in praise of God. This arrangement of the books of the Psalms can be seen as follows.

Preface	Psalms 1–2
Book I	Psalms 3–41
Book II	Psalms 42–72
Book III	Psalms 73–89
Book IV	Psalms 90–106
Book V	Psalms 107–145
Final "Hallel"	Psalms 146–150

Psalms 1 and 2 provide the beginning of the frame of the Book of Psalms. Psalm 1 is a wisdom poem, contrasting the two fundamental options for all human beings—choosing righteousness in accord with God's law, or wickedness in opposition to God's law. The two parts of Psalm 1 contrast the righteous person, who studies God's law and prospers (Psalm 1:1–3), with the wicked person who will not stand in judgment, but will perish (Psalm 1:4–6). Several key words and phrases link this psalm with Psalm 41 at the end of Book I.

Blessed is the man (Psalm 1:1).
> *Blessed is he who considers the poor* (Psalm 41:1).
… his delight is in the law of the Lord (Psalm 1:2).
> *I know that you are pleased with me* (Psalm 41:11).
Therefore the wicked will not stand in the judgment (Psalm 1:5).
> *he will not rise again from where he lies* (Psalm 41:8).

The phrases "blessed is the man," "blessed are they," and "blessed is the nation" occur about thirty times in the Psalms. In the New Testament, Jesus will comment on these passages, when He reveals who are truly blessed. His Sermon on the Mount proclaims: "Blessed are the pure in heart, for they shall see God" (Matthew 5:8). The Beatitudes seem to complete the thought begun in Psalm 1. Those who obey God's law and accept His invitation to conversion and entry into the kingdom of God are truly and profoundly blessed.

Psalm 2 moves from rebellious individuals to rebellious nations. There are several links with the preceding psalm. That the wicked will perish is pronounced in both psalms. *The way of the wicked will perish* (Psalm 1:6). *Serve the Lord with fear, with trembling* *rejoice, lest he be angry, and you **perish** in the way; for his wrath is quickly kindled* (Psalm 2:11–12). Psalm 1 begins with *Blessed is the man …[whose] delight is in the law of the Lord* (Psalm 1:1–2), whereas Psalm 2 ends with *Blessed are all who take refuge in him* (Psalm 2:12b). Those who take refuge in the Lord and meditate on the law of the Lord are blessed, in contrast with the wicked who will experience God's wrath and ultimately perish.

The kings of the earth appear in Psalm 2: *The kings of the earth set themselves… against the Lord and his anointed* (Psalm 2:2). This verse is applied to Jesus in Acts 4:26–27. The back of the frame of the psalter, the grand "Hallel" also speaks to the kings of the earth. While the kings of the earth are conspiring in wickedness in Psalm 2, the kings are called to praise the Lord in Psalm 148. *Kings of the earth and all peoples, princes and all rulers of the earth! Young men and maidens together, old men and children! Let them praise the name of the Lord, for his name alone is exalted; his glory is above earth and heaven* (Psalm 148:11–13).

Judgment emerges in Psalm 1. *Therefore the wicked will not stand in the judgment* (Psalm 1:5). God's judgment appears again in Psalm 149. *Let the high praises of God be in their throats and two-edged swords in their hands, to wreak vengeance on the nations and chastisement on the peoples, to bind their kings with chains and their nobles with fetters of iron, to execute on them the judgment written! This is glory for all his faithful ones* (Psalm 149:6–9).

The two introductory psalms invite the individual to make a fundamental choice to follow God and obey His commands. Blessedness, or happiness, comes from one's relationship with the Lord. *Happy is he whose help is the God of Jacob, whose hope is in the Lord his God* (Psalm 146:5). Every living person desires happiness. No one wants to live a life of misery or meaninglessness. No one wants to perish. Every one wants to be blessed by God. *The Lord takes delight in those who fear him, in those who hope in his steadfast love* (Psalm 147:11). Psalms foster and enable individual and group prayer to God.

Psalms are for the most part poetical: they employ language in a special way, to express what everyday language can hardly say. Often careful and prayerful reading brings to light some element in the poetry of the psalms that allows entering into a deeper relationship of prayer with God on the path the psalmist uncovered. The reader can follow that path: repeatability was probably the reason why the prayerful poems were included in the Book of Psalms.

A puzzling aspect of Psalm 3, for instance, is that the psalmist is at ease at first, and yet asks for deliverance later on. Some have tried to explain this by assuming that the psalmist is in the Temple of Jerusalem (holy mountain) awaiting the decision of the Lord to whom he has entrusted his case. So, while his enemies are outside, he can spend a restful night in the precincts of the Temple. This explanation presumes much that is not expressed in the text of the psalm and seems therefore rather questionable.

Another and better explanation offers itself when we are more attentive to the poetic form. The situation presented by the psalm implies an inter-play of three: the psalmist, God, and the group of adversaries. The praying person is both the subject and the object of actions concerning his enemies; he is also both subject and object of actions concerning God, but the adversaries are only the object of divine actions, they are never the subject of an action of which God would be the object. This asymmetry is significant: God is on the side of the psalmist in a special way, but the adversaries never address God.

The interrelationships are best understood starting from the words that indicate something of space, like "round about me" or "against me." We can easily imagine the praying person surrounded by a multitude of adversaries who stand all around him in a complete circle and who rise up in order to attack him; but there is a second circle around the praying person: The Lord is as a shield all around him in order to defend him, so that he can peacefully lie down even when the enemies rise for the attack.

The contrasts are strong: the enemies **rise** against the psalmist, but the Lord **raises** His head and **strikes down** the enemies, so that the psalmist **lies down** in peace. The awaking symbolizes the victory for the psalmist. The image of an attacking army has literally shaped the form of the psalm. The text moves from the outside towards the center and back as follows. It starts with the outer ring of enemies against the psalmist (Psalm 3:1–2), then arrives at the inner circle which is God protecting the psalmist (verse 3), and reaches the center: man's cry for help and God's answer (verse 4). From this point onward the tension that has been built by these different relationships is resolved in reversed order. First the psalmist is sustained by God (verse 5), then follows his relationship with the adversaries (verse 6). He is not afraid. Lastly come man's cry and God's reply (verse 7), which logically should come in the middle in verse 5, but has been postponed in order to heighten the effect. The psalm's conclusion extends the experience of the psalmist to all the people in verse 8.

Consider this diagram:

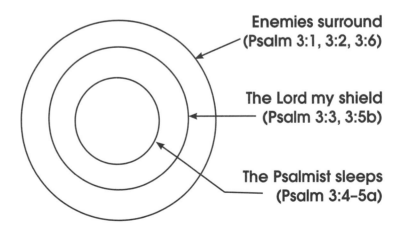

The easiest way to understand Psalm 3 is to begin in the middle at the point of view of the speaker. He addresses the Lord directly with "You" giving three titles to God: *shield – glory – lifter of my head* (Psalm 3:3). These titles correspond to the three actions, which the psalmist is said to do: *lie down – sleep – awake*. The three titles of God in fact give the grounds for the three actions of the praying person since the Lord sustains him. The link between these titles and the human actions made possible by them appears in verse 4. The psalmist calls on the Lord, and God answers. Neither the way of calling on God, nor His answer is given. The outer circle shows the enemies in relation to God.

Psalm 3:1	Enemies rise against me.	Psalm 3:6	I do not fear the enemies.
		Psalm 3:7	God rises.
Psalm 3:2	They say there is no help.	Psalm 3:8	God delivers (saves).

The central theme of divine salvation is introduced with a negative statement in the mouth of the adversaries: "there is no help for him in God" (Psalm 3:2). This is resolved in the end of the psalm when the Lord brings deliverance and blessing to His people. A remarkable fact is that the enemies constantly refer to God as "God" while the speaker only uses the more personal name "Lord." This is an indication that the personal relationship of the psalmist with the Lord is the basis for the salvation, which comes from the Lord.

A Christian application of the psalm emerges in Matthew 27:43 where Psalm 3:3 is quoted. See also Psalm 22:8–9. Seen against the background of Psalm 3 the mockers of Jesus at the Crucifixion are in the same situation as the enemies of the psalmist. God will eventually strike them down and raise up the praying person, His Son. A further link with the Crucifixion is found in Psalm 3:8: *Your blessing be upon your people,* reminds strongly of *"Father forgive them"* (Luke 23:34). Finally an application of Psalm 3:6 to Jesus Crucified completes the picture. If the mockers quote Psalm 3 with the words of the enemies, then their opponent (Jesus) must be the same as the speaker of the psalm to whom it applies that he will lie down, sleep and rise up (from the dead), because the Lord sustains him.

> Between heaven and earth a channel of communication is established in which the action of the Lord meets the hymn of praise of the faithful. The liturgy unites the two holy places, the earthly temple and the infinite heavens, God and man, time and eternity. During the prayer, we accomplish an ascent towards the divine light and together experience a descent of God who adapts himself to our limitations in order to hear and speak to us, meet us and save us … Hence it is necessary to discover and to live constantly the beauty of prayer and of the liturgy. We must pray to God with theologically correct formulas and also in a beautiful and dignified way.
> Pope John Paul II, *Psalms & Canticles*
> (Chicago: Liturgy Training Publications, 2004), pp. 227–228

1. Find some common concepts in these psalms.

Psalm 1:1–3	
Psalm 146:5–9	
Psalm 1:4–6	
Psalm 146:9b	
Psalm 2:1–2	
Psalm 148:11–13	

2. How and when were the psalms collected? CCC 2585

3. What do the psalms commemorate and what do they anticipate? CCC 2586

4. Identify some things that the words of the psalmist do. CCC 2587

5. Describe the characteristics of the "blessed" or happy person. Psalm 1:1–3

6. Compare the beginning and end of Book I of the Psalms.

Psalm 1:1	
Psalm 2:11b	
Psalm 41:1b	
Psalm 1:6a	
Psalm 41:11–12	

7. Where could you find peace? Psalm 3:3–6; 4:7–8

* Share a time in your life when God gave you peace.

8. Identify some characteristics of God.

Psalm 5:1–3	
Psalm 5:7	
Psalm 6:9	
Psalm 7:10–11	
Psalm 8	

9. Find some psalms in Book I (Psalms 1–41) to pray in these situations.

Healing from illness and suffering	
Deliverance from enemies	
Help in evil times	
Wisdom to know God's ways	
Deliverance from fear	
Forgiveness of sins	

10. Where can you find joy? Psalm 16:5, 11

11. What does the psalmist ask in Psalm 17:8?

12. Why does the psalmist thank God in Psalm 18?

13. Where can you see God's glory?

Psalm 19:1–6	
Romans 1:19–20	
Psalm 19:7–10	

14. What can you learn from these verses?

Psalm 22:1	
Isaiah 49:14; 54:7	
Matthew 27:46	
Psalm 22:19	

15. Memorize Psalm 23 to use in a time of trouble.

16. Write your favorite verse of confidence from Psalm 27.

17. Find the comfort in Psalm 30:5, 11.

18. What happens to the person who will not confess his sin? Psalm 32:3–4

19. Describe the person who is forgiven by God. Psalm 32:1–2, 5–11

20. Write your own prayer poem, a psalm of praise to God.

CHAPTER 6

Psalms Books II & III
Psalms 42–72 and 73–89

O God, you are my God, I seek you, my soul thirsts for you;
my flesh faints for you, as in a dry and weary land where no water is.
So I have looked upon you in the sanctuary, beholding your power and glory.
Because your merciful love is better than life, my lips will praise you.
So I will bless you as long as I live;
I will lift up my hands and call on your name.
Psalm 63:1–4

The Bible contains its own hymnal: the Psalter, which was not only born from the practice of singing and playing musical instruments during worship but also contains by itself—in the practice, the live performance—essential elements of a theory of music in faith and for faith. We must pay attention to the place of this book in the biblical canon in order to appreciate its significance properly. Within the Old Testament the Psalter is a bridge, as it were, between the Law and the Prophets. It has grown out of the requirements of the temple cult, of the law, but by appropriating the law in prayer and song it has uncovered its prophetic essence more and more. It has led beyond the ritual and its ordinances into the "offering of praise," the "worldly offering" with which people open themselves to the Logos and thus become worship with him. In this way the Psalter has also become a bridge connecting the two Testaments. In the Old Testament its hymns had been considered to be the songs of David; this meant for Christians that these hymns had risen from the heart of the real David, Christ. In the early church the psalms are prayed and sung as hymns to Christ. Christ himself thus becomes the choir director who teaches us the new song and gives the Church the tone and the way in which she can praise God appropriately and blend into the heavenly liturgy.

Pope Benedict XVI, *A New Song for the Lord*
(New York: Crossroad Publishing, 1996), pp. 122–123

The prayer book of the Church changes in a subtle way as it moves into Book II. The psalms in Books II and III address God with the Hebrew word *Elohim* (God) much of the time, whereas the other books of the Psalter use the Hebrew *YHWH Yahweh* (the name of God revealed to Moses in Exodus 3:14 often read as Lord) the majority of the time. These distinctions were first noticed in the books of the Torah, the Pentateuch. It has become customary to refer to one sacred author as the "Elohist," and the other as the "Yahwist." The Elohist bent is most clearly and frequently seen in Books II and III. Another interesting aspect of this part of the Psalter is that God speaks in oracles to His people in some of the psalms, so there is a dialogue between God and man.

God speaks to His people in prophetic oracles in several psalms. *"Be still and know that I am God. I am exalted among the nations. I am exalted in the earth!"* (Psalm 46:10) is an example of this type of oracle. In Psalm 50:7–23, God explains what He expects from His people. God doesn't need sacrifices or offerings, but He expects thanksgiving and right living from His people. *"He who brings thanksgiving as his sacrifice honors me; to him who orders his way aright I will show the salvation of God!"* (Psalm 50:23). In Psalms 81 and 82, God implores His people to abandon their false idols and return to the God who delivered them from bondage in Egypt. God also asks for justice to be shown to the weak and the needy. He expects justice and mercy from His people.

Eleven psalms in Books II and III of the Psalter are attributed to the "Sons of Korah." Korah was one of the Levitical priests descending from Levi's son Kohath (Exodus 6:16–24). While Israel wandered in the desert, Korah rebelled against Moses and Aaron. The earth swallowed up Korah as a result of his rebellion against God's anointed (Numbers 16:32–35). But, some of the sons of Korah survived and much later the descendants of Korah led the singing in praise of God as a victory march for the armies of Israel (2 Chronicles 20:19–21).

Psalms 42, 44–49, 84, 85, 87, and 88 are ascribed to the sons of Korah. The poetry of the sons of Korah is breathtakingly beautiful. *As a deer longs for flowing streams, so longs my soul for you, O God* (Psalm 42:1). *How lovely is your dwelling place, O Lord of hosts!…For a day in your courts is better than a thousand elsewhere. I would rather be a doorkeeper in the house of my God than dwell in the tents of wickedness* (Psalm 84:1, 10). The sons of Korah long to return to the temple of the Lord.

Asaph, another Levitical priest, was a descendant of Levi's son Gershom (1 Chronicles 6:33–39). Asaph was a musician appointed by David to be in charge of the songs in the house of the Lord. Twelve psalms name Asaph in their headings—Psalms 50 and 73–83, and all of them are found in this section of the Psalter. Among the most beautiful verses attributed to Asaph are: *Whom have I in heaven but you? And there is nothing upon earth that I desire besides you. My flesh and my heart may fail, but God is the strength of my heart and my portion forever* (Psalm 73:25–26). The descendants of Asaph continued in the musical tradition of their forefather. One hundred forty-eight priestly singers, sons of Asaph, were listed among those who returned from the Babylonian exile (Nehemiah 7:44).

Music was important to David and remains important in the worship of God. A pure and holy God deserves the highest form of worship and the most melodious form of praise that can be offered to Him. "In this regard, the Christian community must make an examination of conscience so that the beauty of music and hymnody will return once again to the liturgy. They should purify worship from ugliness of style, from distasteful forms of expression, from uninspired musical texts which are not worthy of the great act that is being celebrated" (Pope John Paul II, ibid. *Psalms and Canticles*, p. 228).

There are several types of psalms in the Psalter—hymns of praise, thanksgiving, wisdom psalms, royal psalms, historical psalms, and laments. The largest individual category, more than a third of the psalms in the Psalter could be classified as psalms of lament. And, in Books II and III of Psalms, over half are psalms of lament. In some cases, the psalmist cries out to God in anguish, feeling abandoned by God (Psalms 42–44, 60, 74, 77, 85, 88–89). *I say to God, my rock: "Why have you forgotten me? Why do I go mourning because of the oppression of the enemy?"* (Psalm 42:9).

In other psalms of lament, the psalmist cries out to God for deliverance from a desperate situation (Psalms 54–59, 61, 64, 69, 79, 80, 83, and 86). The emotion expressed in these psalms is heart wrenching. *My heart is in anguish within me, the terrors of death have fallen upon me. Fear and trembling come upon me, and horror overwhelms me* (Psalm 55:4–5). *Be merciful to me, O God, be merciful to me, for in you my soul takes refuge; in the shadow of your wings I will take refuge, till the storms of destruction pass by* (Psalm 57:1). The psalmist often asks God to take a stand against his enemies, and the language is often vengeful.

Psalms of lament are written in a six-part structure. Whether the psalm is long or rather short, these elements of structure and style can usually be identified.

1) An invocation of God's holy name
2) A description of the current problem or pressing need
3) A plea for help or deliverance from God
4) A justification for the reason God should send help
5) A vow to offer sacrifice when the petition is granted
6) Thankful praise to God for the deliverance expected

The elements of the psalm of lament may not always follow in perfect order, but all of the six parts can usually be identified. Some psalmists spend more time explaining their need and others use more verses to describe how wicked the enemies behave. Some express emotions of human anger and frustration. Often God is asked to punish the enemies. Psalm 54 provides a good example for study.

1) Invocation	*Behold God is my helper; the Lord is the upholder of my life*	Psalm 54:4
2) Problem	*For insolent men have risen against me, ruthless men seek my life;*	Psalm 54:3
3) Plea	*Save me, O God, by your name, and vindicate me by your might.*	Psalm 54:1
4) Reason	*For you have delivered me from every trouble, and my eye has looked in triumph on my enemies*	Psalm 54:7
5) Vow	*With a freewill offering I will sacrifice to you;*	Psalm 54:6
6) Thanks	*I will give thanks to your name, O Lord*	Psalm 54:6

One of the most famous prayers for mercy in the Psalter is found in this section. Psalm 51, also known as the *Miserere*, is prayed in the Liturgy of the Hours every Friday as part of Morning Prayer. The heading, or superscription for Psalm 51 attributes it to David when Nathan the prophet confronted him after his adultery with Bathsheba. The Miserere demonstrates confession and repentance. This is a psalm of lament begging God for mercy and forgiveness.

It would be difficult to pray Psalm 51 and not be moved to remorse for one's own sin and the sins of the world, which so offend a good and holy God. The ways in which sin separates a person from God and robs him of joy and gladness are portrayed clearly. The same sentiments expressed by a sinner thousands of years ago continue to resound in the penitent cries of sinners today. The plea of the sinner begs to be restored to God's grace and to once again experience the joy of salvation and the presence of the Holy Spirit.

The Miserere, one of the most famous prayers of the Psalter, the most intense and commonly used penitential psalm, the hymn of sin and pardon [is] a profound meditation on guilt and grace.

Psalm 51 outlines two horizons. First, there is the dark region of sin in which man is placed from the beginning of his existence: *Behold in guilt I was born, a sinner was I conceived* (Psalm 51:7). Even if this declaration cannot be taken as an explicit formulation of the doctrine of original sin as it was defined by Christian theology, undoubtedly it corresponds to it: indeed, it expresses the profound dimension of the innate moral weakness of the human person…

If, however, man confesses his sin, the saving justice of God is ready to purify him radically. Thus we come to the second spiritual part of the psalm, the luminous realm of grace. By the confession of sins, for the person who prays there opens an horizon of light where God is at work. The Lord does not just act negatively, eliminating sin, but recreates sinful humanity by means of his life-giving Spirit: he places in the human person a new and pure "heart," namely, a renewed conscience, and opens to him the possibility of a limpid faith and worship pleasing to God.

"Even if our sins were as black as the night, divine mercy is greater than our misery. Only one thing is needed: the sinner has to leave the door to his heart ajar … God can do the rest … Everything begins and ends with his mercy," so writes Saint Faustina Kowlaska.

Pope John Paul II, *Psalms and Canticles*
(Chicago: Liturgical Training Publications, 2004), pp. 64–66

1. Find some oracles in the psalms in which God is speaking.

Psalm 46:10	
Psalm 50:5ff	
Psalm 75:2–5	
Psalm 81:6ff	
Psalm 82:2–5	

2. List some of the forms of prayer found in the Psalter. CCC 2588

3. For whom are Psalms 45 and 72 sung?

4. Describe some of the imagery in Psalm 42.

5. Write your favorite verses from Psalm 51.

6. Write your own penitential psalm to God. (See Psalms 32 and 51 for ideas.)

7. Who quoted Psalms in the New Testament, and for what purpose?

Psalm 2:7	Acts 13:33	
Psalm 8:5–7	Hebrews 2:6–8	
Psalm 52:3–5	John 3:19–20	
Psalm 53:2–3	Romans 3:10–12	
Psalm 110:1	Matthew 22:44	

8. Who can the following verses describe?

Psalm 55:12–14	Matthew 26:21–24	
Psalm 69:9	John 2:16–17	

9. The sons of Korah wrote eleven psalms. What can you learn about Korah?

Who was Korah?	Exodus 6:16–24	
What did Korah do?	Numbers 16:29ff	
Who survived?	Numbers 26:11	

10. Select your favorite "sons of Korah" psalm. Psalms 42, 44–49, 84–85, 87–88

11. What can you learn about Asaph and Heman? 1 Chronicles 15:15–19

12. Choose your favorite psalm attributed to Asaph. Psalms 50, 73–83

13. What main sentiments are expressed in Psalm 62?

Psalm 62:1–2	
Psalm 62:5–8	
Psalm 62:11–12	

14. What historical events are recalled in these Psalms?

Psalm 78:43–51	
Psalm 68:7–8	
Psalm 78:13–14	
Psalm 78:15	
Psalm 78:23–25	
Psalm 78:26–29	

15. Choose two favorite verses in Psalm 84.

16. What does Psalm 89 celebrate?

17. How does Book III of the Psalms end? Psalm 89:52

18. Identify the components of a Psalm of lament from Psalm 80.

Invocation	
Problem or need	*We are the scorn of our neighbors. Psalm 80:6* *You are angry with us and ignore our prayers. Ps 80:4* *We are broken and ravished. Psalm 80:12–13*
Plea for help	
Reason God should help	
Vow to sacrifice	
Thankful praise to God	

19. and 20. Compose your own psalm of lament below.

Invocation	
Problem or need	
Plea for help	
Reason God should help	
Vow to sacrifice	
Thankful praise to God	

Monthly Social Activity

This month, your small group will meet for coffee, tea, or a simple breakfast, lunch, or dessert in someone's home. Pray for this social event and for the host or hostess. Try, if at all possible, to attend.

After a short prayer and some time for small talk, reflect on your study of the psalms. Psalms is the prayer book of the church. How do you pray regularly? Is God inviting you to go deeper.

Examples

◆ *I make sure I go to Mass every Sunday. I arrive early and I remain after the priest has left the altar to make my thanksgiving to God.*

◆ *My husband and I pray the rosary together in the car when we are traveling.*

◆ *Each day, I try to take a short time of prayer, to give my day to the Lord and to listen for His guidance.*

CHAPTER 7

Psalms Books IV & V
Psalms 90–106 and 107–150

O sing to the LORD a new song;
Sing to the LORD, all the earth!
Psalm 96:1

I will extol you, my God and King,
and bless your name for ever and ever.
Every day I will bless you,
and praise your name for ever and ever.
Great is the LORD, and greatly to be praised,
and his greatness is unsearchable.
One generation shall laud your works to another,
and shall declare your mighty acts.
Psalm 145:1–4

The analysis of the oft-repeated imperative *psallite* (sing) in the psalms thus allows us to draw a few concrete conclusions about possible biblical directives for music in the Church. This imperative runs through all of Scripture; it is the concrete version of the call to worship and glorify God, which is revealed in the Bible as the most profound vocation of human beings. This means that musical expression is part of the proper human response to God's self-revelation, to his becoming open to a relationship with us. Mere speech, mere silence, mere actions are not enough. That integral way of humanly expressing joy or sorrow, consent or complaint, which occurs in singing is necessary for responding to God, who touches us precisely in the totality of our being. In the course of this discussion we have seen that the word *psallite* entails more than "to sing;" it does not necessarily require instrumental accompaniment, but because of its origin it does refer to instruments in which, as it were, creation is made to sound. Admittedly the biblical adaptation of this word has made singing—that is, making music vocally—primary.

Pope Benedict XVI, *A New Song for the Lord*
(New York: Crossroad Publishing, 1996), p. 126

The Yahwist author of Sacred Scripture returns in dominance for Books IV and V of the Psalter with a preference for referring to God as *YHWH*, or Lord. Book IV begins with a moving psalm of lament attributed to Moses. Psalm 90 contrasts human frailty and the brevity of man's life with the eternity of God. Man returns to dust, but God is from everlasting to everlasting. The psalmist acknowledges that man's days are short, but that God has existed before the earth was formed and will live forever. Dante alludes to Psalm 90 in the *Divine Comedy — Purgatorio.*

The psalms make for interesting reading. But, they must be more than beautiful poems to be read. Pope Benedict XVI encourages the faithful to sing the psalms and worship God with them. Singing, praising, and worshiping God draw people up into the fulfillment of the responsibility of children of God to praise Him. Psalm 91 possesses beautiful imagery *You will not fear the terror of the night, nor the arrow that flies by day … A thousand may fall at your side, ten thousand at your right hand; but it will not come near you* (Psalm 91:5–7). There could be found no greater psalm of comfort than Psalm 91, which is used often in funeral liturgies.

However, Psalm 91 has also been used in other ways, apart from song and worship. Satan quoted Psalm 91:11–12 in his attempt to tempt Jesus (Matthew 4:6; Luke 4:10–11). Satan suggested that Jesus throw Himself down from the parapet of the temple, to see if God would send angels to rescue Him. But, Jesus responded with Sacred Scripture, *"You shall not put the Lord your God to the test"* (Deuteronomy 6:16). The psalms are written for prayer and praise to God, not for debate, argumentation, or temptation.

Israel was awaiting a Messianic King, who would deliver them from their troubles. Royal psalms appear in this section, which highlight God's divine kingship and majesty (Psalm 93, 95–99).

Psalm 93:1	*The Lord reigns; he is robed in majesty.*
Psalm 95:3	*For the Lord is a great God, and a great King above all gods.*
Psalm 96:6	*Honor and majesty are before him;* *strength and beauty are in his sanctuary"*
Psalm 97:1	*The Lord reigns; let the earth rejoice.*
Psalm 98:6	*With trumpets and the sound of the horn* *make a joyful noise before the King, the Lord!*
Psalm 99:4	*Mighty King, lover of justice, you have established equity;* *you have executed justice and righteousness in Jacob.*

Historical psalms recount God's faithfulness to Israel throughout salvation history. There are five historical psalms, four of which occur in these last books of the Psalter (Psalm 78, 105, 106, 135, and 136). These psalms were probably instrumental in helping the Chosen People to recall God's marvelous deeds and recount the history of Israel to their children, from generation to generation. Because these psalms were sung, the youth could receive a history lesson while at the same time sing their psalms of praise and thanksgiving to God.

Wisdom psalms, by their form and content, show similarities with other poems in the wisdom literature of the Bible. They use proverbs, similes and metaphors, instructions from a parent to a child, or a teacher to a student, and even acrostics. Acrostic poems begin each line of the psalm with a successive letter of the Hebrew alphabet. Acrostic psalms are Psalms 9–10, 25, 34, 37, 111, 112, 119, and 145. Psalm 119 is stylistically unique in that each line of a stanza begins with the same repeated Hebrew letter. The Hebrew alphabet has 22 characters and the English alphabet has 26 letters. So, a word-for-word translation, preserving the acrostic form would be impossible. However, Monsignor Ronald Knox used a paraphrase to compose acrostic psalms in English, skipping the K, X, Y, and Z.

Psalm 111 [112 in RSVCE]

A blessed man is he, who fears the Lord,
Bearing great love to his commandments.
Children of his shall win renown in their country;
Do right and thy sons shall find a blessing.
Esteem dwells with such a man, and great prosperity;
Fame shall ever record his bounty.
Good men see a light dawn in darkness;
His light, who is ever merciful, kind and faithful.
It goes well with the man who lends in pity;
Justice shall be found in all his pleadings.
Length of days shall leave him still unshaken;
Men will remember the name of the just for ever.
No fear shall he have of evil tidings;
On the Lord his hope is fixed unchangeably.
Patient his heart remains and steadfast,
Quietly he waits for the downfall of his enemies.
Rich are his alms to the needy;
Still, through the years his bounty abides in memory.
The Lord will lift up his head in triumph,
Ungodly men are ill content to see it.
Vainly they gnash their teeth in envy;
Worldly hopes must fade and perish.

The Holy Bible,
translated by Monsignor Ronald Knox
(New York: Sheed and Ward, 1950)

Hymns of praise celebrate the grandeur and power of God in creation and in His work in salvation history. Hymns of praise follow a three-part structure. First, there is an invitation to worship the Lord and praise His name. Second, the body of the psalm provides the reason for worship and describes some of the attributes of the Lord, or the mighty works by which God has made Himself known. Finally, the psalm concludes with a recapitulation of the beginning and reinforces how good it is to praise the Lord and give glory to His name.

Songs of Ascent appear in Psalms 120–134 of this section. Pilgrims on their way to the temple in Jerusalem may have passed the time, singing songs on their journey. All sojourners on earth are on pilgrimage in this life. It is far better to continue on this journey in a spirit of song and praise, rather than in discouragement and drudgery. Songs of praise lift the spirit and point hearts and minds to God.

The Passover Hallel, or Egyptian Hallel,- encompasses Psalms 113–118. These are Hallelujah psalms, which reflect on the Exodus experience of Israel and are used in the Jewish Passover service, or Seder. Jesus, Mary, and Joseph, and all faithful Jews would have sung these psalms as part of their worship. Mary uses Psalm 113:7–8 in her Magnificat before the Angel Gabriel (Luke 1:46–55). And of the hundreds of Old Testament quotes found in the New Testament, one-third are, from the Psalter.

Hallelujah psalms have the word Hallelujah in them. *Hallelujah* is Hebrew for "Praise the Lord," or "Praise God." Some psalms which have the word Hallelujah explicitly in the title are Psalms 111–113, 117, 135, 146–150.

It may indeed be said that the purpose of the psalms is to turn the soul into a sort of burning bush, into a vague replica of the one which God used to make His presence felt to Moses. For if God found nothing better for that purpose than a burning bush, the soul itself ought to catch fire in order to communicate with God. ... The praying of the psalms should promote the kind of fire in the soul that even in its greatest intensity is controlled by moderation. Whenever one finds the psalmist exploding, one should be keenly conscious of Paul's instruction that the man of God should never lose patience (2 Timothy 4:2) even when he has to reprove, and regardless of how much he has to endure in the process. That he has to endure, among other things, the perspective of very harsh contrasts inseparable from salvation history is the very point of Psalm 1, which itself is a summary of all the other psalms.

Stanley L. Jaki, *Praying the Psalms*
(Grand Rapids, MI: Eerdmans, 2001), pp. 27–28)

Take time to sing a joyful song to the Lord. Praise God, thank God for your blessings, extol His glory and lament when times are dark. God inhabits the praises of His people. The person who sings a psalm to God is happy and blessed.

1. What can you learn from the following verses?

Psalm 90:1–2	
Psalm 90:4	
Psalm 90:9	
Psalm 90:10	

2. Where are you in the span of days? How can you number them? Psalm 90:9–12

3. Choose two favorite verses from Psalm 91.

4. What type of psalm is Psalm 92?

5. Identify some historical events from Psalms 95, 105, and 106.

Psalm 95:8–10	
Psalm 105:7–11	
Psalm 105:16–22	
Psalm 105:26–37	
Psalm 106:6–12	
Psalm 106:13–23	

6. Choose a favorite royal psalm of Divine Kingship. Psalms 93, 95–99

7. Select two favorite verses from Psalm 103 and paraphrase them.

8. How does Book IV of the Psalms end? Psalm 106:48

9. What is the main idea of Psalm 107?

10. Identify some musical instruments in Psalm 108.

11. Compare the following verses.

Psalm 111:10	
Proverbs 9:10	
Sirach 1:16–20	

* Who is the wisest person you know? Who would you consult about a problem?

12. What concept do you find in the following verses?

Psalm 116:3	
Psalm 116:8	
Psalm 116:15	

*Have you ever experienced the death of a close loved one? Do you fear death?

13. Find the shortest and longest psalms in the Bible. Look at Psalms 110–120.

14. How should a believer feel about death? 1 Corinthians 15:51–58

15. Choose three favorite verses from Psalm 119.

16. Write your favorite "Song of Ascents" from Psalms 120–134.

17. Find a short intercession in Psalm 141:3.

18. List some constant characteristics of the Psalms. CCC 2589

19. Identify the three components of a psalm of praise using Psalm 113.

Invitation to worship and praise the Lord.	*Praise the Lord!* *Praise, O servants of the Lord,* *Praise the name of the Lord!*
Reason for worship. Attributes of the Lord.	
Recapitulation. How good it is to praise the Lord.	*Praise the Lord!*

20. Write your own psalm of praise to the Lord below.

Invitation to worship and praise the Lord.	
Reason for worship. Attributes of the Lord.	
Recapitulation. How good it is to praise the Lord.	

CHAPTER 8

The Value of Wisdom
Proverbs 1–9

The fear of the Lord is the beginning of wisdom
Proverbs 9:10a

Trust in the Lord with all your heart,
and do not rely on your own insight.
In all your ways acknowledge him,
and he will make straight your paths.
Proverbs 3:5–6

Keep your heart with all vigilance;
for from it flow the springs of life.
Proverbs 4:23

The Book of Proverbs in Hebrew is titled *Mishle Shelomoh,* or "The Proverbs of Solomon." The word *mishle* can mean sayings, proverbs, comparisons, and analogies. Proverbs is a compendium of brief, mostly two-line wisdom sayings (Proverbs 10–29), framed by a longer poetic set of instructions at the beginning (Proverbs 1–9), and some longer sayings and poems at the end (Proverbs 30–31). Proverbs are clever, pithy, rhythmic sayings that are easy to remember and they pass on traditional wisdom. Proverbs aim to transmit practical wisdom to youth. They can be seen as a parent teaching a child, or a teacher instructing a student.

There are maxims and adages in every culture. Parents might say, "Birds of a feather flock together," to warn their children not to associate with a bad crowd. "Early to bed and early to rise makes a man healthy, wealthy, and wise," encourages good disciplinary habits. "The early bird gets the worm" promotes promptness and industry. "Put aside something for a rainy day," advises frugality and prudence in financial matters. There may be societal sayings and instructions specific to a family or region. Have you ever been told, "Always wear clean underwear; you may end up in an emergency room?"

An editor probably compiled several centuries of folk sayings into the final manuscript of Proverbs. Solomon and other kings of Israel fostered the collection of traditional wisdom. Parts of the book (Proverbs 22–24) resemble an Egyptian work from the eleventh century BC, called "The Wisdom of Amenemophis." Some of the sayings may have come from northern Arabia, if Agur is from Massa in the east beyond Edom (Proverbs 30). So, Proverbs is probably an anthology of Hebrew wisdom from the time of Solomon in the tenth century BC to the time of Nehemiah in the fifth century BC. Proverbs may have been used as a textbook for well-bred young men training for diplomatic service.

What is a proverb? While almost everyone can recognize a folk saying or adage when they hear one, it may be more difficult to agree on a definition. Some characteristics of the proverb include (1) brevity, (2) cleverness, (3) practical truth, (4) moral lesson, (5) memorable form, (6) common wisdom, and (7) traditional source of origin. Most would agree that one distinguishing feature of a proverb is its origin in the common lore of a people over the years. It falls into the common domain of a society, which is shared by everyone but attributed to no one in particular. In contrast, an *aphorism* is a clever saying coined by a specific person or well-known literary figure. "The unexamined life is not worth living" is an aphorism attributed to Socrates (469–399 BC).

Adults use proverbs to pass on the wisdom of elders to the next generation. Parents and teachers want to help youth to grow in wisdom and goodness. Experience is a good but painful teacher. Embracing the wisdom of the elders, the young person can avoid evil and the pitfalls of foolishness. Attaining wisdom early can enable the person to live a joyful life and to avoid unnecessary adversity.

The invitation to pursue wisdom — Proverbs 1–9 presents the purpose of this book, the call to seek wisdom. A father makes an impassioned plea to his son to hear, to listen, to heed, to not forget, and to trust in the Lord. Wisdom is the revelation of the living God, the fountain of life. Wisdom gives discernment, which is essential for a moral act: saying and doing the right thing at the right time for the right reason. *The fear of the Lord is the beginning of wisdom* (Proverbs 9:10). This fear is not synonymous with terror or fright, but rather a healthy respect and awe. Sailors and fishermen "fear the sea." They love the sea as an integral part of their livelihoods. But, they know from experience that a storm can brew in an instant, causing devastation. So, they respect the times and seasons, and the signs of changing weather. In a similar way, the wise person recognizes the power and majesty of God, and develops love and a reverent awe of God.

> Love the holy Scriptures, and wisdom will love you. Love wisdom, and she will keep you safe. Honor wisdom, and she will embrace you.
> Saint Jerome (AD 347-420), *Corpus Scriptorum,* 56.3.201

Wisdom is the revelation of God, who brings life. Wisdom is the Word of the living God, who makes His word known (Proverbs 1:23), so that a person can come to conversion. Faith is required for conversion. *Trust in the Lord with all your heart* (Proverbs 3:5), shows the way to faith. Faith involves trusting in the Lord, in His goodness and mercy. The wise person trusts that the Lord has a perfect plan for his or her individual life. *My son, if you receive my words and treasure up my commandments with you, making your ear attentive to wisdom ... then you will understand the fear of the* LORD *and find the knowledge of God* (Proverbs 2:1–2, 5). The father wants his child to trust God, to seek wisdom, and to obey the commandments in order to have life. The father knows that evil leads to trouble, suffering, and death.

Lady Wisdom emerges as the personification of wisdom in Proverbs 1, 8, and 9. She cries aloud in the streets and admonishes the scoffers and fools who hate knowledge. Even though she calls out, the dullards refuse to listen. Then, when calamity comes upon the unwise, they will panic, but it will be too late. Wisdom will not come to the aid of the foolish. *Because they hated knowledge and did not choose the fear of the LORD …[they] are killed by their turning away* (Proverbs 1:29, 32). Wisdom reveals that God gives each person a choice in life. Everyone has a free will to choose God or to reject Him. Choosing God puts one on the path to life. Rejecting God, choosing evil, sets one on a path toward death.

Proverbs 8 indicates that wisdom originates in God. Lady Wisdom reveals that, *The Lord created me at the beginning of his work, the first of his acts of old* (Proverbs 8:22). The person who chooses God and wants to walk in His ways will also want to seek after wisdom. *For he who finds me [wisdom] finds life, and obtains favor from the Lord; but he who misses me injures himself; all who hate me love death* (Proverbs 8:35–36). Proverbs 9 shows Lady Wisdom building her house with seven pillars. She slaughters beasts and mixes wine for a great banquet. The house symbolizes the school of wisdom, and the banquet represents her teaching. The house with its seven pillars can also be seen as the world. Look at the painting on the cover of this book.

In contrast to Lady Wisdom is another feminine personification, Dame Folly, who is sometimes seen as an adulteress and other times as foolishness. *You will be saved from the loose woman, from the adventuress with her smooth words, who forsakes the companion of her youth and forgets the covenant of her God; for her house sinks down to death, and her paths to the shades; none who go to her come back nor do they regain the paths of life* (Proverbs 2:16–19). This figure has several layers of meaning. The adulteress also represents idolatry in Israel.

The concern of intermingling and intermarrying with foreign women was the issue of idolatry. Solomon was led into sin by his foreign wives who turned his heart away from fidelity to the One True God to the worship of false gods (1 Kings 11:1–13). Idolatry and adultery are both grave sins against a pure and holy God. The foolish and seductive woman appears again and again in the verses of Proverbs. The wise and loving father continues to warn his son to avoid her. *Let not your heart turn aside to her ways, do not stray into her paths; for many a victim has she laid low; yes, all her slain are a mighty host. Her house is the way to Sheol, going down to the chambers of death* (Proverbs 7:25–28).

Proverbs begins with a father's impassioned plea to his son to seek out wisdom. Lady Wisdom warns the foolish and those who reject divine wisdom that their end will be death. Since folly is a characteristic of childhood, to mature one must learn to forsake foolishness and strive after wisdom, which is a gift of God. The fool is mentioned nineteen times in Proverbs. The fear of the Lord is the primary virtue, which predisposes one to attaining other virtues: humility, prudence, justice, and charity. Pride is a major obstacle to wisdom and virtue. *When pride comes, then comes disgrace; but with the humble is wisdom* (Proverbs 11:2).

Many themes run through this section of Proverbs. The father wants his son to fear the Lord and to seek wisdom. There are many blessings that wisdom can bestow. Lady Wisdom warns against wickedness and foolishness. Two paths or two choices are presented. Fidelity to God, and seeking after wisdom brings life and blessing. Following Dame Folly, the seductress, leads to death and destruction. One path leads to light and life, the other leads to darkness and death. One path is straight and honest, the other is crooked and devious.

The Book of Proverbs extols the virtues of hard work and perseverance. Many practical admonitions are given against laziness, against becoming surety for a neighbor, against loose speech, dishonesty, and adultery. The basic message is to love and to trust God and to obey His commandments. *The fear of the Lord is the beginning of wisdom, and the knowledge of the Holy One is insight* (Proverbs 9:10). The person who loves and trusts God will seek after wisdom. And God desires to grant the gift of wisdom to those who seek Him with a pure heart. *I love those who love me, and those who seek me diligently find me. Riches and honor are with me, enduring wealth and prosperity. My fruit is better than gold, even fine gold, and my yield than choice silver* (Proverbs 8:17–19).

We find in the *sapiential* (wisdom) Books of the Old Testament certain texts, which exalt the role of Wisdom that existed prior to the world's creation. Passages such as the one from Psalm 90 should be interpreted in this sense: *Before the mountains were brought forth, or ever you had formed the earth and the world, from everlasting to everlasting you are God* (Psalm 90:2); or passages like this one that speaks of the creator Wisdom: *The LORD created me at the beginning of his work, the first of his acts of old. Ages ago I was set up, at the first, before the beginning of the earth* (Proverbs 8:22–23). The praise of Wisdom, contained in the Book of the same name, is also evocative: *She reaches mightily from one end of the earth to the other, and she orders all things well* (Wisdom 8:1).

The sapiential texts themselves which speak of the eternal pre-existence of Wisdom, also speak of the descent, the abasement of this Wisdom, who pitched a tent herself among men. Thus we already hear echoing the words of the Gospel of John, who speaks of the tent of the Lord's flesh. He created a tent for himself in the Old Testament … Saint Paul, in developing his Christology, refers precisely to this sapiential perspective: in Jesus he recognizes the eternal wisdom that has always existed, the wisdom that descends and pitches a tent for herself among us and thus he can describe Christ as *the power of God and the wisdom of God* (1 Corinthians 1:24), he can say that Christ has become, through God's work, *our wisdom, our righteousness and sanctification and redemption* (ibid, 30). Similarly, Paul explains that Christ, like Wisdom, can be rejected … so that within God's plans a paradoxical situation is created, the Cross, which was to transform itself into the means of salvation for the whole human race.

Pope Benedict XVI, *General Audience*, October 22, 2008

1. What can you learn from the following passages?

Proverbs 1:7	
Proverbs 2:5–6	
Proverbs 3:5–6	
Proverbs 9:10	

2. Describe the appropriate relationship to one's parents.

Proverbs 1:8–9	
Proverbs 4:1	
CCC 2214	
CCC 2216	

3. What practice is encouraged in these verses?

Exodus 34:26	
Proverbs 3:9–10	
Malachi 3:10	

* How generous are you to the Lord, the Church, and the poor?

4. Who should a wise person avoid?

Proverbs 1:10–19	
Proverbs 2:11–17	
Proverbs 4:14–19	

* Who is the wisest prominent person in society today? What is the smartest thing you've done?

5. How can you appropriate these verses to your life?

Proverbs 3:1	
Proverbs 4:4	
Proverbs 6:20–23	
Proverbs 7:1–3	
Deuteronomy 6:1–8	

6. Why should you desire discipline?

Proverbs 3:11–12	
Hebrews 12:5–11	

* How can you learn to accept discipline and correction better?

7. Who is described in these verses? Check a New American Bible translation.

Proverbs 9:13–18	
Proverbs 14:1b	

8. Who is personified in the following passages?

Proverbs 1:20–33	
Proverbs 2:13–20	
Proverbs 4:5b–9	
Proverbs 8:1–36	
Proverbs 9:1–12	

9. In the Catholic liturgy, who is acclaimed as the "Seat of Wisdom?" CCC 721

10. Who is the perfection of God's wisdom and power? 1 Corinthians 1:24b–25

11. What happens to those who seek wisdom? Proverbs 8:17; 9:11

12. List some warnings from Proverbs 5.

13. What instruction is given from nature in Proverbs 6:6–11?

14. Identify six things that the Lord hates. Proverbs 6:16–19

15. What advice is given in these verses?

Proverbs 4:24	
Proverbs 6:2–3, 12	
James 3:5–10	
James 3:17–18	

* How can you make your speech become a blessing to others?

16. Find some warnings in these verses.

Proverbs 6:24–35	
Proverbs 7:5–27	

17. How much should you desire wisdom? Proverbs 8:10–11

18. List four things that wisdom has. Proverbs 8:14

19. What does wisdom offer? Proverbs 8:18–21; 9:11–12

20. What happens to those who find wisdom? Proverbs 8:32–36

CHAPTER 9

Proverbs of Solomon
Proverbs 10–22:16

The plans of the mind belong to man,
but the answer of the tongue is from the LORD.
All the ways of a man are pure in his own eyes,
but the LORD weighs the spirit.
Commit your work to the LORD,
and your plans will be established.
Proverbs 16:1–3

The Proverbs attributed to Solomon are presented in poetic, artistic beauty. There are paradigms, models, examples, riddles, metaphors, and similes. The imagery is crisp and timeless. The messages and morals are as clear today as they were thousands of years ago. The language is breathtakingly beautiful and easy to commit to memory. Proverbs are clever sayings that convey truths in a short and pithy manner. The moral emerges compellingly from the poetry. There are several styles of biblical wisdom poetry that will be evident in these passages.

Parallelism involves the use of balanced lines. Many of the sayings in the Book of Proverbs are fashioned according to classic Hebrew poetry. Parallelism is an aspect of biblical poetry using two parts to each verse in balanced lines. In some cases, the second half of the verse will complement the first. However, in other cases, the second line will contrast with the first.

* Synonymous Parallel — Both lines of the verse mean the same thing, or very near the same meaning. *The fear of the Lord is the beginning of wisdom,*
     and the knowledge of the Holy One is insight (Proverbs 9:10).
* Antithetic Parallel — Contrast in the second line of the verse provides the antithesis of the first line. *A soft answer turns away wrath,*
     but a harsh word stirs up anger (Proverbs 15:1).
* Synthetic Parallel — A desired action is presented, with an expected outcome following in the next line. *Commit your work to the Lord,*
     and your plans will be established (Proverbs 16:3).
* Comparisons — A natural phenomenon, which would be common to all, is followed by a behavioral analogy. *Like cold water to a thirsty soul,*
     so is good news from a far country (Proverbs 25:25).
* "Better than" comparisons — A weighted value is placed on a concept to show the preferred stance. *Better is a little with the fear of the Lord,*
     than great treasure and trouble with it (Proverbs 15:16).

Reading large sections of the Book of Proverbs at one sitting can be very helpful in understanding the message that the Sacred authors and the Holy Spirit intend to convey.

Sometimes a theme is being developed with increasing emphasis. However, there are several themes that pop up time after time, seemingly out of nowhere. The warnings against involvement with a seductress or adulteress woman appear with a regular frequency. Perhaps the warnings against idolatry and sexual sins should be repeated frequently in society today as well.

Many interesting and diverse poetic devices are also used for effect.

* Rhetorical Question — An orator speaks in such a way that the meaning is implied. A question is posed, but the answer is implicit and understood.
    Who has woe? Who has sorrow? Who has strife? (Proverbs 23:29).
* Irony — This mode of speech expresses a meaning contrary to that which the speaker intends to convey, or that which will bring about a usually expected or desired outcome. *The sluggard buries his hand in the dish;*
    it wears him out to bring it back to his mouth (Proverbs 26:15).
* Hyperbole — In rhetoric, hyberbole is a figure of speech, which expresses much more or less than the truth. It represents things as much greater or less than, or far better or worse than they really are. Hyberbole is, in essence, an exaggeration of the truth for effect. *For her house sinks down to death,*
    and her path to the shades (Proverbs 2:18).
* Puns — A pun uses the same word in different senses. It could be a play on words, which may be difficult to translate from one language or culture to another.
    When your eyes light upon it [wealth], it is gone;
    for suddenly it takes to itself wings,
    flying like an eagle toward heaven (Proverbs 23:5).
* Alliteration — Alliteration repeats the same letter of the alphabet at the beginning of two or more words immediately succeeding each other, or at short intervals. Alliteration is very difficult to convey in translation. In English, "Sister Suzy sat upon a thistle" or "Peter Piper picked a peck of pickled peppers," are clear examples of alliteration.   A *faithful witness does not lie, but a false witness*
    breathes out lies (Proverbs 14:5) comes close.
* Chiasmus — A type of antithesis presents the second half of a verse balanced against the first. *Such are the ways of all who get gain by violence;*
    it takes away the life of its possessors (Proverbs 1:19).

Numerical sayings are also composed. Sometimes counting can help a person remember important details. This is especially common in teaching children. And so, Proverbs uses numerical sayings, like the one below.
    There are six things which the Lord hates,
        seven which are an abomination to him:
    haughty eyes, a lying tongue,
        and hands that shed innocent blood,
    a heart that devises wicked plans,
        feet that make haste to run to evil,
    a false witness who breathes out lies,
        and a man who sows discord among brothers (Proverbs 6:16–19).

Acrostic poems use each letter of the Hebrew alphabet for the first letter of each successive line of the poem. The Hebrew alphabet has twenty-two characters, whereas, the English alphabet has twenty-six letters. So, it is virtually impossible to translate a word-for-word rendering of an alphabetical poem from Hebrew into English. Here, Monsignor Ronald Knox produced an alphabetic rendering by paraphrasing Proverbs 31:10–31, and skipping the Q, X, Y, and Z.

THE PRAISE OF A GOOD WIFE

A man who has found a vigorous wife has found a rare treasure, brought from distant coasts.

Bound to her in loving confidence, he will have no need of spoil.

Content, not sorrow, she will bring him as long as life lasts.

Does she not busy herself with wool and thread, plying her hands with ready skill?

Ever she steers her course like some merchant ship, bringing provision from far away.

From early dawn she is up, assigning food to the household, so that each waiting-woman has her share.

Ground must be examined, and bought, and planted out as a vineyard, with the earnings of her toil.

How briskly she girds herself to the task, how tireless are her arms!

Industry, she knows, is well rewarded, and all night long her lamp does not go out.

Jealously she sets her hands to work; her fingers clutch the spindle.

Kindly is her welcome to the poor, her purse ever open to those in need.

Let the snow lie cold if it will, she has no fears for her household; no servant of hers but is warmly clad.

Made by her own hands was the coverlet on her bed, the clothes of lawn and purple that she wears.

None so honoured at the city gate as that husband of hers, when he sits in council with the elders of the land.

Often she will sell linen of her own weaving, or make a girdle for the traveling merchant to buy.

Protected by her own industry and good repute, she greets the morrow with a smile.

Ripe wisdom governs her speech, but it is kindly instruction she gives.

She keeps watch over all that goes on in her house, not content to go through life eating and sleeping.

That is why her children are the first to call her blessed, her husband is loud in her praise.

Unrivalled art thou among all the women that have enriched their homes.

Vain are the winning ways, beauty is a snare; it is the woman who fears the Lord that will achieve renown.

Work such as hers claims its reward; let her life be spoken of with praise at the city gates.

The Holy Bible, translated by Ronald Knox
[New York: Sheed and Ward, 1950]

Children are inherently impulsive and self-centered. They are not, by nature, interested in fairness or social justice. Parents must teach their children to share their toys or treats with other children. Saint Thérèse of Lisieux recounts in her autobiography that an older sister offered to give Thérèse some of her treasured things. When asked to choose, Thérèse said, "I choose all." She wanted everything! She was a typical selfish child, who God transformed into a saint.

The Book of Proverbs highlights the importance of family life and the primary role of the father in training up his children in the ways of the Lord. The wise parent teaches his child how to think and to control his passions. The parent draws upon his own experience to teach the child the importance of faith, correct reason, wisdom, understanding, and obedience to God's commandments in order to live a joyful, faithful, productive life.

Augustine was raised in a home with a Christian mother and a pagan father. He spent an entire year of his adolescence in idleness, to the detriment of his soul. When ultimately confronted with the truths of the Gospel, he found it challenging to set aside the life of debauchery and those illicit pleasures that were his routine. Before accepting Baptism, Augustine needed to set aside his mistress and make arrangements for the care of the illegitimate son he had fathered.

> There seethed all around me a cauldron of lawless loves … I hated myself for wanting not. I sought what I might love, in love with loving … To love then, and to be loved, was sweet to me, but more when I obtained to enjoy the person I loved. I defiled, therefore, the spring of friendship with the filth of concupiscence, and beclouded its brightness with the hell of lustfulness.
> Saint Augustine of Hippo (AD 354–430), *Confessions*, 3.1.1

How did Augustine change from a narcissistic young man into a believing Christian, and ultimately a bishop and saint? What compelled a young man to abandon the path of foolishness and to seek the fullness of truth and the call to wisdom, righteousness, and sanctity?

> "What moved the heart of the young African rhetorician, skeptic and downhearted, and what impelled him to definitive conversion was not above all Ambrose's splendid homilies (although he deeply appreciated them). It was rather the testimony of the Bishop and his Milanese Church that prayed and sang as one intact body."
> (Pope Benedict XVI, *General Audience*, October 24, 2007)

Each person should seek after wisdom and beg God for the gift of wisdom. And when that gift is given, it can and should be passed on to the young, the young in years as well as the new Christians in our midst. Pray that the witness of the Church might attract the young and those who desire the wisdom of God.

1. Find some common truths in the following passages.

Proverbs 10:4–5	
Proverbs 12:11, 14	
Proverbs 12:24	

2. Explain Proverbs 10:1.

3. Define the virtue found in Proverbs 14:8a and CCC 1806.

4. What grave sin must be avoided?

Proverbs 11:2	
Proverbs 16:5, 18	
Proverbs 21:4	
CCC 1866	

5. Compare the following verses.

Proverbs 10:12	
1 Peter 4:8	

6. Identify something to be desired.

Proverbs 12:1	
Proverbs 13:24	
Proverbs 22:6	
Sirach 30:1–13	

* Describe a well-disciplined child or adult you know.

7. Explain Proverbs 11:22 in your own words.

8. What does Scripture say about a good wife?

Proverbs 12:4	
Proverbs 18:22	
Proverbs 19:14	

9. Explain the seriousness of the sin described in these verses.

Proverbs 14:5	
Proverbs 19:9	
CCC 2476	

10. What can you learn from these passages?

Proverbs 10:11–31	
Proverbs 12:17–23	
Proverbs 13:3	
Proverbs 15:1–2	

11. Find some other references to the tongue in Proverbs.

Proverbs 16:21–24	
Proverbs 17:27	
Proverbs 18:4, 21	
Proverbs 21:23	

12. Do you agree with Proverbs 28:6?

13. Who does a righteous man bless? Proverbs 20:7

14. Describe a righteous man you know.

15. What is better than riches? Proverbs 22:1

16. What does Proverbs say about wealth?

Proverbs 10:21–22	
Proverbs 11:24–25	
Proverbs 13:11, 22	
Proverbs 15:6	
Proverbs 19:4–6	

17. Find some comparisons.

Proverbs 15:16–17	
Proverbs 16:8; 17:1	
Proverbs 21:9	

18. What can you learn about making plans?

Proverbs 19:21	
CCC 303	

19. Choose your favorite proverb from Proverbs 10–22:16.

20. Share a proverb that you learned from your parents or grandparents.

CHAPTER 10

Sayings of the Wise
Proverbs 22:17–31

Incline your ear, and hear the words of the wise,
and apply your mind to my knowledge;
for it will be pleasant if you keep them within you,
if all of them are ready on your lips.
That your trust may be in the LORD,
I have made them known to you today, even to you.
Proverbs 22:17–19

The sayings of the wise in this section, even though there are similarities with the Egyptian *Teachings of Amenemophis,* are directed specifically to believers, those who trust in the Lord and fear Him. True wisdom is a gift from God and God's grace is necessary to appropriate wisdom into virtuous behavior. Can a pagan who has no interest or belief in God be a moral and righteous person? Is it necessary to know God and to receive His grace and blessing in order to grow in virtue?

> But you, most bitter enemies of grace that you are, oppose us with examples of impious men, "who," you say, "though strangers to faith, abound in virtues in which, without the help of grace, there is only the good of nature, granted that it is enslaved by superstitions. Such men," you say, "by the powers alone of their innate liberty, are frequently found to be merciful and modest and chaste and sober." But when you say this, only see: you have already taken away what you should attribute to the grace of God: namely the effectiveness of will …*Whoever says the impious man is righteous, cursed shall he be among the people and hated among the tribes* (Proverbs 24:20–24), — how much better, I say, if you were to confess that even these virtues that you find in them are the gifts of God.
>
> Saint Augustine (AD 354–430), *Contra Iulianum,* 4.3.16

No matter how wise a person may be, it will do him very little good if he lacks the grace and fortitude to conform his will to his knowledge. Faith in God disposes the soul to seek wisdom and knowledge. Early in the Book of Proverbs, the son was told, *Trust in the Lord with all your heart, and do not rely on your own insight. In all your ways acknowledge him, and he will make straight your paths* (Proverbs 3:5–6). Moreover, repeatedly the young are told, *The fear of the Lord is the beginning of wisdom, and the knowledge of the Holy One is insight* (Proverbs 9:10). Even if a person has the grace and character formation to behave righteously, it will benefit him more if he knows Whom to thank for the grace he has received to grow in virtue and wisdom. In every culture, people must be trained to reign in their passions and impulses in order to become good and righteous.

There is a secular adage that says, "Alexander the Great conquered the then know, world, but Alexander the Great could not conquer Alexander." Despite his military prowess, Alexander the Great was an alcoholic. Alcohol controlled Alexander and ultimately led to his untimely demise. The same could be said of countless other talented individuals in every age, who achieved greatness, but then fell into disgrace due to severe and uncontrolled character weaknesses and serious sin patterns.

Various themes recur throughout the sayings in Proverbs. Two sections frame the Book of Proverbs—one at the beginning and another at the end. The major theme is the faithfulness of God and the need for righteous living. The frame at the beginning presents a father talking to his son and the frame at the end could be a mother teaching her daughter about the traits necessary to become an ideal wife. Irrespective of one's age or status, the sayings in the book present wisdom for all people of any age, who want to grow in wisdom and virtue before God.

Fear the Lord and obey the commandments. The admonition to fear the Lord, to trust the Lord and to obey the Lord is repeated over a dozen times in Proverbs. The necessity of keeping the commandments is also stressed repeatedly. *Let your heart hold fast my words; keep my commandments and live* (Proverbs 4:4). The contrasting images of light and darkness, and life and death appear in the sayings. The patrimony of the wisdom literature is adopted by the Christians and can also be found in the teaching of the Twelve Apostles.

> There are two ways, one of life and one of death …The way of life is this: first, you shall love God, who created you; second your neighbor as yourself. Whatever you would not wish to be done to you, do not do to another …You shall not murder. You shall not commit adultery. You shall not seduce boys. You shall not commit fornication. You shall not steal. You shall not practice magic. You shall not use potions. You shall not procure abortion, nor destroy a newborn child. You shall not covet your neighbor's good. You shall not perjure yourself. You shall not bear false witness. You shall not speak evil. You shall not bear malice. You shall not be double-minded or double-tongued; for a double tongue is the snare of death.
> *Didache or Teaching of the Twelve Apostles* (AD 140), 1.1, 2.1

Interestingly, Proverbs has at least thirty-five sayings relating to speech, or warnings about the tongue. Many are negative admonitions to avoid lying (Proverbs 6:17–19), crooked speech (Proverbs 6:12), excessive speech (Proverbs 10:19), rash words (Proverbs 12:18), foolish talk (Proverbs 14:3), harsh words (Proverbs 15:1), gossiping (Proverbs 20:19), cursing father or mother (Proverbs 20:20), and exalting oneself or bragging (Proverbs 30:32). Proverbs gives many warnings and cautions against the sins of the tongue and the foolishness of the loose tongue. These admonitions are as relevant today as they were centuries ago. The battle to train and tame the tongue is a life-long task, not merely a task for youth. Many adults need to also heed the admonitions to soften their speech. But, there is also positive instruction for good speech and the use of the tongue to bless others and to share wisdom and encouragement.

> *He who guards his mouth preserves his life* (Proverbs 13:3).
> *The lips of the wise spread knowledge* (Proverbs 15:7).
> *The words of the pure are pleasing to him* (Proverbs 15:26b).
> *Pleasant words are like a honeycomb* (Proverbs 16:24).
> *He who restrains his words has knowledge* (Proverbs 17:27).
> *He ... whose speech is gracious,*
>   *will have the king as his friend* (Proverbs 22:11b).
> *A word fitly spoken is like*
>   *apples of gold in a setting of silver* (Proverbs 25:11).

Any wise person would be known for his or her positive speech. The fool indulges in loose speech, bragging, harsh words, lying, gossiping, and cursing. These negative and sinful speech patterns can become habits that are very difficult to break. For the person who seeks to become wise, God's grace is available to help to tame the tongue.

Pride and lack of self-control are also addressed in Proverbs. *A man without self-control is like a city broken into and left without walls* (Proverbs 25:28). Self-control is a virtue that is not found in overabundance in contemporary society, nor is humility. *When pride comes, then comes disgrace; but with the humble is wisdom* (Proverbs 11:2). Humility is a virtue that brings its own reward, and acknowledges that God is the giver of all good gifts. Whatever is admirable or noble has come from above. Humility is the antithesis of pride, the root of all sin. *Pride goes before destruction, and a haughty spirit before a fall* (Proverbs 16:18). There are countless examples of this phenomenon. *A man's pride will bring him low, but he who is lowly in spirit will obtain honor* (Proverbs 29:23).

Industry is praised, while slothfulness is abhorred in Proverbs. The sluggard should observe the tenacity of the ant and avoid excessive slumber and laziness, which brings on poverty (Proverbs 6:6–11). Laziness causes poverty, but diligence brings about prosperity. *He who tills his land will have plenty of bread, but he who follows worthless pursuits has no sense* (Proverbs 12:11).

Warnings against gluttony and drunkenness appear in these passages. *Be not among winebibbers, or among gluttonous eaters of meat; for the drunkard and the glutton will come to poverty, and drowsiness will clothe a man with rags* (Proverbs 23:20–21). The people in ancient times had no knowledge of the disease of alcoholism or the problem of obesity. Yet, excessive alcohol consumption and overeating have brought suffering to humanity for all time. The wise person seeks God's grace and an appropriate means of developing self-control in these areas.

Wealth and poverty recur in many sayings. There are also warning about loans and being surety for one's neighbor. Perhaps the best proverb is one that encourages contentment with whatever one has. *Give me neither poverty nor riches; feed me with the food that is needful for me, lest I be full, and deny you, and say, "Who is the Lord?" or lest I be poor, and steal, and profane the name of my God* (Proverbs 30:8–9). Wealth should be honestly attained, with a desire to leave something for one's heirs.

Discipline is essential for life with the Lord. Many passages encourage parents to discipline their children. The Lord disciplines the son whom he loves (Proverbs 3:11–12), and parents who love their children should do likewise. *He who spares the rod hates his son, but he who loves him is diligent to discipline him* (Proverbs 13:24). Various child-rearing philosophies have surfaced in recent times. The truth of the biblical wisdom is proven whenever one encounters a well-disciplined and well-mannered child. Self-discipline is also encouraged. *Whoever loves discipline loves knowledge, but he who hates reproof is stupid* (Proverbs 12:1).

A wise person must strive to get his temper under control. *A man of quick temper acts foolishly, but a man of discretion is patient* (Proverbs 14:17). One who cannot control his temper displays weakness of character. *He who is slow to anger is better than the mighty, and he who rules his spirit than he who takes a city* (Proverbs 16:32).

Women hold prominence of place in Proverbs. Lady Wisdom and Dame Folly appear inviting people to follow them. A good wife is credited as a gift or favor from the Lord (Proverbs 18:22), whereas a nagging or quarreling wife is as annoying as a continual dripping of rain (Proverbs 19:13). In the beginning of Proverbs, the father encourages his son to rejoice in the wife of his youth (Proverbs 5:18–19), and to avoid the adulterous woman. There are many admonitions to avoid the harlot, loose woman, evil woman, and adulteress (Proverbs 2:16–19; 5:3–8, 5:20; 6:24–35; 7:5–27; 22:14; 23:27–28; 30:20; 31:3).

Lady Wisdom appears in the opening of the book in Proverbs 1–9 as a sort of frame for the sayings to follow. The end of the frame appears in the perfect wife described in Proverbs 31:10–31 at the close of the book. Perhaps a Hebrew mother would teach these verses to her daughter, as she taught the Hebrew alphabet to her. Moreover, these passages may convey more than just a picture of a good wife. Proverbs 31:10–31 may direct our thoughts to Lady Wisdom once again, now in action—prudent, understanding, diligent, self-controlled, kind, considerate, hard-working, fruitful, and caring for the poor and needy. The key to this pericope can be found near the end. *Strength and dignity are her clothing and she laughs at the time to come. She opens her mouth with wisdom, and the teaching of kindness is on her tongue* (Proverbs 31:25–26).

Proverbs provides a wonderful tool to teach wisdom to the young. It can also prove an excellent examination of conscience for the not-so-young to evaluate how well they are appropriating God's wisdom in the maturing years. Fear of the Lord, self-discipline, proper speech, industry, the right use of wealth, food and drink, and obedience to the commandments provide reflection for people of all ages.

1. What is the purpose of the sayings and admonitions? Proverbs 22:17–21

2. Find some practical wisdom in the following verses.

Proverbs 25:9–10	
CCC 2489	

3. Describe proper speech. Proverbs 25:11

4. Identify the sin in the following verses.

Proverbs 20:1	
Proverbs 23:20–21	
Proverbs 23:29–35	
Proverbs 31:4–5	

5. What sin can be found in Proverbs 23:1–3, 20–21?

6. What virtue opposes the above sins? CCC 1809

7. Identify a virtue compared in Proverbs 16:32 and 25:28.

8. What can you learn from these passages?

Proverbs 14:17, 29	
Proverbs 15:18	
Proverbs 16:29	
Proverbs 22:24–25	

9. How can one develop self-control? 1 Corinthians 10:13

10. Identify a serious sin in Proverbs 20:20.

11. Why is the above sin so serious? Exodus 20:12

12. How can you show honor to your family members?

13. What are some responsibilities of parents toward children?

Proverbs 22:6; 23:13	
Proverbs 29:17	
CCC 2221, 2223	
CCC 2225	
CCC 2226	

14. Explain the wisdom in Proverbs 27:2.

15. Compare the following verses.

Proverbs 28:13	
1 John 1:9–10	

16. Explain Proverbs 31:7–9.

* Describe the virtue of contentment. Are you content with your life?

17. Write one of the numerical proverbs. Proverbs 30:7–23

18. Compare the following verses referring to Lady Wisdom.

Proverbs 8:8–12	
Proverbs 31:26–27	

19. Choose five favorite characteristics of the "good wife." Proverbs 31:10–31

20. What characteristic of wisdom would you like to improve in your own life?

Chapter 11

Reflections on Life
Ecclesiastes 1–6

I have seen the business that God has given to the sons of men to be busy with.
He has made everything beautiful in its time;
also he has put eternity into man's mind,
yet so that he cannot find out what God has done from the beginning to the end.
Ecclesiastes 3:10–11

Teacher of Israel — In the third century BC, there was a wisdom teacher in Jerusalem who was known as *Qoheleth,* "Preacher." He must have been a rather successful and authoritative teacher with students. The name is curious because its grammatical form indicates a function or title rather than a proper name. The name is used seven times in the Book of Ecclesiastes (Ecclesiastes 1:1, 1:2, 1:12; 7:27; and 12:8, 12:9, 12:10). The name Qoheleth always indicates the authorship of the sayings that have been collected in the book. Usually it is others who refer to the preacher using this name. But, just once in Ecclesiastes 1:12, the teacher speaks of himself by this name. This shows that the name was not just given to him by others, but that it was actually a kind of title. In later centuries, when the gatherings of people were structured in what became the synagogue, the title had already fallen into disuse.

The name of the teacher Qoheleth is related to the noun *qa'ha'l,* meaning "the gathering of the people" (Ecclesiastes 12:6; Psalm 22:23). The cognate verb *qa'hal* usually means "to come together in a meeting" (Leviticus 8:4), but it is never used in the sense of "to gather." Both the noun and the verb have something to do with Israel as a people, an aspect which the Latin *Ecclesiastes* tries to convey. Most likely the title indicates a certain type of leadership. The words he spoke and left in writing for the congregated people outlasted him. They were collected, prefixed with a title, and concluded with an editorial note (Ecclesiastes 12:9–14), indicating that they were considered normative for later generations.

A first reading of the book can be unsettling, as the author wrestles with the meaning of life and asks a lot of hard questions but finds few answers. As a believer in God, *Qoheleth* struggles with the injustice and dishonesty he observes. As a result, life appears to have little value. In all his deliberations on life, human behavior, the natural and social order, and even faith in God, he seems to find only meaninglessness. One can easily understand why initially the Jews, and later Christians, questioned the inspired status of Ecclesiastes. Ultimately however, this apparent negative outlook on life is seen not as skepticism or agnosticism, but rather a sobering realism—man is not the master of life!

The book begins with *The words of the Preacher (Qoheleth), the son of David, king in Jerusalem* (Ecclesiastes 1:1). The most remarkable son of King David, reigning immediately after him in around the tenth century BC was, of course, Solomon. Those books in Sacred Scripture in the wisdom tradition always connect themselves in some way with Solomon's wisdom, even though this book was probably written about 700 years later. Qoheleth seems to ponder some sayings of Solomon and wrestles with the unfairness and inconsistencies in life.

Historical Background — To understand the Book of Ecclesiastes, a review of the historical situation of Palestine in the Hellenistic period is helpful. For a long time, the political scene of the Ancient Middle East had been dominated by a succession of several vast empires. The Assyrian (740–610 BC), Babylonian (610–540 BC), and Persian (540–331 BC) empires each had an influence on Israel. The Persians brought an end to Israel's exile in Babylon around 539 BC. The Persian Empire lasted so long and seemed so stable that its laws were considered to be irrevocable (Daniel 6:8). Nevertheless, it ended abruptly when Alexander the Great started a long military campaign (334–323 BC), which took him from his homeland in Macedonia into the Middle East as far as Egypt and India. With a well-trained army and strategic genius, he subdued most of the Middle East in less than a decade. When Alexander died, his generals (*Diadochs*) wrestled for control, and in the end his empire was divided into three Hellenistic states:

- ✳ The Ptolemaic kingdom in Egypt and Palestine,
- ✳ The Antigonid empire in Greece, and
- ✳ The Seleucids in Mesopotamia and Persia.

These Hellenistic monarchies were not a continuation of the Greek tribal kingship, nor of the Eastern tyrannical rule. Rather a new kind of leadership emerged. A ruler—Greek, Jew, Syrian or Lydian, would have his own autonomy. This personal kingship ideology usually had a religious aspect and more often than not Hellenistic rulers might be called "savior" or "benefactor." The Hellenistic period formally ended with the death of Cleopatra in 30 BC, when the last Hellenistic monarchy was incorporated into the Roman Empire.

In the political turmoil of the third and second centuries BC all the great civilizations of the Middle East were influenced by Greek (Hellenistic) culture. More in cities than in rural areas, Hellenism brought many changes. Language changed most acutely. Aramaic, which had been universally used in the Persian Empire, was replaced by a new common language: Koine–Greek. This common language enhanced the development of geography, historiography, astronomy, medicine, and philosophy. Technology leapt forward. National boundaries were no longer of utmost importance. Local deities lost their prominence and even something like a common religion emerged. In this cosmopolitan situation, the all important and fundamental question of good and evil was addressed in a variety of new ways. A characteristic philosophy of the time, *stoicism*, held that wisdom consisted in knowing and living according to the rational nature of the world (the logos of the cosmos). Others held that the matter of good and evil was a mere social construct, and that one therefore should follow the prevailing opinions.

All of these new influences impacted the Jews, first in the diaspora but then also in Palestine. Initially many Jews had no qualms about these changes. Technology made life easier and more comfortable. But, cultural assimilation occurred so quickly that soon most Jews outside Palestine could no longer understand the Torah or Prophets in Hebrew. So, the entire Old Testament was translated into Greek for the Greek-speaking Jews. This Greek Bible, called the *Septuagint,* also served to make many non-Jews familiar with Judaism. At first, Hellenism did not impact the Jews in Jerusalem much, since they were situated in a somewhat isolated location. But after the Seleucids took over control of Palestine from the Ptolomees around 200 BC, Hellenism made itself felt.

Structure and Style — Any long text needs structure in order to be comprehensible, but Ecclesiastes seems to defy this basic rule of literature. It is evident that Ecclesiastes does not consist of unconnected sayings accidentally put together, as often seem to be the case in the Book of Proverbs, where shorter and longer sections are detectable but the connection between these units remains elusive.

In the absence of an easily detectable overall structure, a good way to guide the reading is to focus on what is often repeated at the beginning and end of smaller sections and what, therefore, probably is part of the main message of the book.

Several core ideas that are characteristic of the flow of thought of Ecclesiastes are:
- ❋ *All is vanity* (Ecclesiastes 1:2; 2:11; 2:17; 3:19; 11:8; 12:8).
- ❋ *This also is vanity* (Ecclesiastes 2:15-26; 4:4-16; 5:10; 6:9; 7:6; 8:10, 8:14).
- ❋ *For everything there is a time* (Ecclesiastes 3:1–17; 7:17; 8:5–6; 10:17).
- ❋ *Under the sun* (Ecclesiastes 1:3–14; 2:11; 2:17–22; 3:16; 4:1–15; 5:13; 5:18; 6:1; 6:12; 8:9–17; 9:3–13; 10:5).

Based on these central concepts, it is possible to glimpse a line of thought and to arrive at a rough approximation of a structure.

Analyzing all his experiences, the Teacher concludes that man is unable to make any change or difference. Man is not the master of his own life. This idea seems to have been expounded twice in the book in a similar manner. Twice a core idea about the reality of this world *under the sun* is put forth, and then an application is made to the human sphere. The first core idea concerns the ephemeral or fleeting condition of life, and the vicissitude or unexpected changes of fortune in a person's life. These unexpected and sometimes sudden change of events affect everyone and even the wisest and most powerful of persons, the king.

The second core idea is an elaboration of the first. The seeming vanity of all things is thought through to its logical conclusion. No longer is the inconstancy of all human things considered, but the fact that change is something constant and permanent. Everything is fleeting, but this transitory state is an unalterable law: everything has its proper time and never rises above its own time. This idea is subsequently shown to be true in its application to all human activities.

The resulting structure of the Book of Ecclesiastes looks like this:

1:1		**Title:** Royal lineage of Ecclesiastes.
1:2–11	A]	**Thesis:** All is vanity. Nothing has lasting value.
1:12–2:26		**Application:** Even the activities of a wise king are in vain.
3:1–4:16	B]	**Thesis:** Everything happens at its appointed time.
4:17–12:8		**Application:** All human activities are limited.
12:9–14		**Conclusion:** Call for a wise way of life.

Two beautifully balanced poems appear in the first part of Ecclesiastes. The first poem feels quite depressing, reflecting the drudgery and repetitive events of life, which seem quite endless and meaningless. The second poem leaves one with a somewhat more hopeful feeling of acceptance in celebrating the seasons of life.

Ecclesiastes 1:2–9	Ecclesiastes 3:1–8

Vanity of vanities, says the Preacher,
   Vanity of vanities! All is vanity.
What does a man gain by all the toil
   at which he toils under the sun?
A generation goes,
   and a generation comes
   but the earth remains for ever.
The sun rises and the sun goes down,
   and hastens to the place where it rises.
The wind blows to the south,
   and goes round to the north;
round and round goes the wind,
   and on its circuits the wind returns.
All streams run to the sea,
   but the sea is not full;
to the place where the streams flow,
   there they flow again.
All things are full of weariness;
   a man cannot utter it;
the eye is not satisfied with seeing,
   nor the ear filled with hearing.
What has been is what will be,
   and what has been done
     is what will be done;
and there is nothing new under the sun.
	For everything there is a season, and
	   a time for every matter
	     under heaven:
	a time to be born, and a time to die;
	a time to plant, and
	   a time to pluck up what is planted;
	a time to kill, and a time to heal;
	a time to break down,
	   and a time to build up;
	a time to weep, and a time to laugh;
	a time to mourn, and a time to dance;
	a time to cast away stones, and
	   a time to gather stones together;
	a time to embrace, and a time to
	   refrain from embracing;
	a time to seek, and a time to lose:
	a time to keep,
	   and a time to cast away;
	a time to tear, and a time to sew;
	a time to keep silence,
	   and a time to speak;
	a time to love,
	   and a time to hate;
	a time for war,
	   and a time for peace.

1. Summarize Ecclesiastes 1:2–11 in your own words.

* Has there been a time in your life when you felt your life was meaningless?

2. What objective did the Preacher set in Ecclesiastes 1:13?

3. What results from striving for knowledge and wisdom? Ecclesiastes 1:18; 2:13

4. List some ways that Qoheleth tried to find satisfaction. Ecclesiastes 2:1–11

5. Compare the ways of the wise with those of the foolish. Ecclesiastes 2:12–19

6. Find a fear expressed in Ecclesiastes 2:20–21.

7. Where does a person find contentment? Ecclesiastes 2:24–25; 3:12–13

8. Write your five favorite couplets from the poem in Ecclesiastes 3:1–8.

* What season of life are you in right now? Do you feel God with you?

9. Describe some of God's gifts and their purpose. Ecclesiastes 3:10–15

10. What caused Qoheleth to become disillusioned? Ecclesiastes 3:16–19

11. What can you learn from these passages?

Ecclesiastes 3:17	
Acts 10:42	
1 Peter 4:4–5	

12. When have you heard the verse in Ecclesiastes 3:20 spoken in church?

13. What injustices are seen in Ecclesiastes 4:1, 7–8?

14. Describe some values of friendship. Ecclesiastes 4:9–12

* Describe your three best friends.

15. Compare the following verses.

Deuteronomy 23:23	
Psalm 50:14	
Ecclesiastes 5:2, 4	

16. What can you learn from these verses?

Ecclesiastes 5:10–17	
1 Timothy 6:10	

* How much time do you spend thinking or worrying about money?

** What could you do instead of worry?

17. What can you learn about dreams?

Genesis 31:10–11	
1 Kings 3:5	
Ecclesiastes 5:3, 7	

18. Identify some frustrations in Ecclesiastes 6:1–9.

19. Who is stronger than man?

Jeremiah 20:7	
Ecclesiastes 6:10	
1 Corinthians 1:25	

20. Answer the questions posed in Ecclesiastes 6:12–13.

* What is the most troubling iniquity you face in life?

Monthly Social Activity

This month, your small group will meet for coffee, tea, or a simple breakfast, lunch, or dessert in someone's home. Pray for this social event and for the host or hostess. Try, if at all possible, to attend.

After a short prayer and some time for small talk, reflect on the questions you have about life. Each person should share about one question that they would like to ask God.

Examples

◆ *Why did You make mosquitoes?*

◆ *How could I please You more?*

◆ *What can people do to get along better?*

Chapter 12

Teacher of Israel
Ecclesiastes 7–12

As you do not know how the spirit comes to the bones
in the womb of a woman with child,
so you do not know the work of God who makes everything.
Ecclesiastes 11:5

Wise Worldview — Ecclesiastes searches for the meaning of life and has arrived at a universal idea about everything "under the sun." He concludes that God gave a certain order to His creation and man is not able to alter it even though everyone keeps trying. Not even the most powerful man, the king, is able to really change the course of human events. He may try to do so by his wealth or his wisdom, but there is nothing really *new under the sun* (Ecclesiastes 1:9–10). In fact, not just the king, but every human being would like to grasp the deepest meaning of life and everything that goes on in the world. This desire itself is something that God has put in every human being (Ecclesiastes 1:13; 3:11). If this desire cannot be fulfilled, then what should one do about it?

What makes a human being wise is the acceptance of his or her creational condition and endowment. This positive attitude toward the inherent limitation of everything under the sun implies a recognition and acceptance of God who is above the sun, in heaven (Ecclesiastes 5:1–2). Whoever puts his or her behavior in accord with this most fundamental idea about God, the world, and man, is wise and will know a measure of happiness in this life. Ecclesiastes then is not primarily concerned about the place of the devout Jew within the Chosen People of God. The Law of Moses and the preaching of the prophets are not explicit themes, neither are God, sin, or Zion. Ecclesiastes' main field of interest is the whole of creation—God created this world and everything in it, and He alone remains in control. This conviction is essentially religious in nature and is also expressed in the Law of Moses and the preaching of the prophets. Therefore, it is correct to say that Ecclesiastes forms part of the tradition of Israel.

Faith instead of fatalism — Ecclesiastes never really engaged in a debate with Hellenistic sages. He chose to write in Hebrew and not in Greek or even in Aramaic, which was the language most spoken in Palestine at the time. Nevertheless, the influence of Hellenism in his book is unmistakable. Relativism abounds. He accepts the increased wealth and technological advancement of the day. And, in his worldview, both the individual and the world-at-large play a more important role than the Jewish people. Even when attributing his book to the national patron of wisdom, King Solomon, he criticizes traditional wisdom and no longer takes for granted that old age equals wisdom. Especially the well-known Deuteronomic system of divine retribution falls victim to his razor sharp analyses. Although mortality becomes painful, for the issue of good and bad is not resolved in this life, as ultimately in Job's case, Qoheleth does not fall into fatalism or rebellion.

The Preacher seems to have found a way to live with his unanswered questions. For him, God's design is inscrutable but also good. Central to his stance is the conviction that man lives in God's presence and is not himself the master of his life. God has endowed each person with one lifetime, whether long or short, each with a measure of creativity and compassion. To those who acknowledge God's inscrutability and do not become obsessed with amassing power or wealth, God *gives wisdom and knowledge and joy* (Ecclesiastes 2:26; 5:18–20).

Underlying the Preacher's disappointment at seeing wickedness among the righteous, and dishonesty where one would expect to find justice, there is a subtle pro-life message. Qoheleth sees beauty in God's plan and gets a glimpse of eternity. *He has made everything beautiful in its time; also he has put eternity into man's mind* (Ecclesiastes 3:11). Since life is God's gift to man, each person has a duty to enjoy the life that God has so graciously given. A contemporary slogan paraphrases: "Life is God's gift to you. What you do with it is your gift to God!"

There were probably sayings in Ecclesiastes' time that were handed down from parents to children by word of mouth. Those sayings exist in every society, including our own. Parents may tell a child, "A bird in the hand is worth two in the bush" or "a stitch in time saves nine." And so the child strives to follow the instructions of the parent. But, then a surprise can occur. The steadfast and faithful worker, the one who got up early and worked diligently and honestly is not rewarded. The industrious, hard working person does not enjoy health, wealth, and wisdom. Why not? The saying doesn't prove true in each and every situation. The person is confused and disillusioned. Perhaps this is the situation that Qoheleth experienced. The wisdom sayings of his ancestors do not provide an absolute guarantee in each situation. So he struggles with them.

Qoheleth extols the importance of friendship in Ecclesiastes 4:9–12. The vocation of marriage should also begin with strong friendship. *A threefold cord is not quickly broken* (Ecclesiastes 4:12). (1) A godly man and (2) a godly woman who enter into a covenant of marriage enlisting (3) God's sacramental grace and help should become a threefold cord that can prevail over those forces that come against them. Friendship and sticking together in the midst of adversity is better than isolating oneself or divisiveness. There is strength in numbers. Community is stronger than individuality. Unity offers greater strength and protection against the enemy than disunity or isolationism. Ecclesiastes discovers that some sayings do indeed prove to be true and reliable.

He who loves money will not be satisfied with money (Ecclesiastes 5:10). Greed can never be satisfied with more, and wealth without contentment is meaningless. It may seem as if the poor have an advantage over the rich (Ecclesiastes 5:11–14), but in fact, true wisdom is the privilege of the believer.

> Untold wealth is not an advantage, far from it! It is better to be poor and to be one with God. The austere voice of an ancient biblical sage, Ecclesiastes or Qoheleth, seems to ring out in this proverb when it describes the apparently identical destiny of every living creature, that of death, which makes frantic clinging to earthly things completely pointless ... A profound blindness takes hold of man if he deludes himself that by striving to accumulate material goods he can avoid death. ... The topic, however, was to be explored by all cultures and forms of spirituality and its essence was expressed once and for all by Jesus, who said: *"Take heed, and beware of all covetousness; for a man's life does not consist in the abundance of his possessions"* (Luke 12:15).
>
> Pope John Paul II, *General Audience*, October 20, 2004.

Ecclesiastes warns about greed and the love of money that Saint Paul will comment further on in his letter to his disciple Timothy. *For the love of money is the root of all evils; it is through this craving that some have wandered away from the faith and pierced their hearts with many pangs* (1 Timothy 6:10). Greed and covetousness have no place in the life of a child of God. Contentment is the virtue that comes against the sin of greed. Once again, Saint Paul will share practical wisdom on how to achieve contentment. *Not that I complain of want; for I have learned, in whatever state I am, to be content* (Philippians 4:11).

The Preacher deals with the frustration of desires. Man toils, yet his appetite is not satisfied (Ecclesiastes 6:7). *He [man[is not able to dispute with one stronger than he* (Ecclesiastes 6:10). Who is stronger than man? God is stronger than man. God knows the answers to the iniquities of life. But, God is not speaking.

Some of Qoheleth's troubles seem to involve women (Ecclesiastes 7:26). Biblical references to Adam and Eve (Genesis 3), David and Bathsheba (2 Samuel 11), and Amnon and Tamar (2 Samuel 13) demonstrate that, from the beginning, women and men have had the power to lure one another away from God's perfect plan and into serious sin, resulting in inexplicable pain and suffering. Often, even innocent people can experience the long-lasting negative consequences of these sins.

God's ways are inscrutable. Qoheleth recalls the wicked going in and out of the holy place (Ecclesiastes 8:10). This ought not be so! Why doesn't God punish the wicked now? Furthermore, there doesn't seem to be justice in this world. *There are righteous men to whom it happens according to the deeds of the wicked, and there are wicked men to whom it happens according to the deeds of the righteous* (Ecclesiastes 8:14). In other words, sometimes, bad things happen to good people. And sometimes, evil people get away with murder. It doesn't seem to be fair. It ought not be so. Why isn't there justice in this world? Why doesn't God punish the wicked now? Why doesn't God reward the deeds of the righteous now?

How then should one live? According to Qohelth, one should live righteously and generously, anyway, even if he doesn't see an immediate reward for his labors, or compensation for his generosity. *Cast your bread upon the waters, for you will find it after many days* (Ecclesiastes 11:1). Be generous to others and God will return the kindness to you in days to come.

Mystery prevails. Still, there are unanswered questions. *As you do not know how the spirit comes to the bones in the womb of a woman with child, so you do not know the work of God who makes everything* (Ecclesiastes 11:5). God does not owe man an answer to all of the questions and riddles of life. There is a certain degree of ambiguity that man must learn to live with. God is mysterious. And yet, Ecclesiastes does believe in God. He trusts that there is a Creator who makes everything and understands the meaning and purpose of all things, even when man doesn't have a clue as to what is happening around him, or why. The inequities in life and the unanswered questions trouble Qoheleth as they trouble all people who ponder and reflect on the meaning of life.

Ecclesiastes seems to totter between despair and hope. As a teacher, he wants to pass on certain words of wisdom to the young. *Rejoice, O young man, in your youth, and let your heart cheer you in the days of your youth; walk in the ways of your heart and the sight of your eyes. But know that for all these things God will bring you into judgment* (Ecclesiastes 11:9). He seems to be advising the youth to do the best he can and follow his best light. Live life as fully as possible, knowing that there is a God in heaven. Time will tell and God will judge.

Faith in God prevents a complete fall into despair and fatalism. No matter how sobering and cynical his observations seem to be, ultimately they lead Qoheleth to cling wholeheartedly to fear of God and the Torah. Ultimately, Ecclesiastes advises others to concentrate on the same focus. *Fear God, and keep his commandments; for this is the whole duty of man* (Ecclesiastes 12:13). In this, the Preacher shows himself to be a true sage in the line of other Old Testament wisdom teachers: *fear of the Lord is the beginning of wisdom* (Proverbs 1:7; Sirach 1:14), and its full measure, its crown and its root (Sirach 1:16; 18:20). Ultimately, God's ways are mysterious. Only God can bring order and meaning to human life. Man is not in charge. God is in control.

> God speaks quietly. But he gives us all kinds of signs. In retrospect, especially, we can see that he has given us a little nudge through a friend, through a book, or through what we see as a failure—even through "accidents." Life is actually full of these silent indications. If I remain alert, then slowly they piece together a consistent whole, and I begin to feel how God is guiding me... Sometimes he remains puzzling to me. In those cases that annoy me I can also feel the presence somewhere of his mystery, his strangeness.
> Pope Benedict XVI (Cardinal Joseph Ratzinger), *God and the World*
> (San Francisco: Ignatius Press, 2002), pp. 18–19

1. Describe some contrasts between wisdom and folly in Ecclesiastes 7:1–29.

2. Compare the following verses.

Ecclesiastes 7:20	
Isaiah 59:1–13	
Romans 3:23	

3. Explain the problem and character faults identified in Ecclesiastes 7:26.

4. Identify warnings from these verses.

Ecclesiastes 7:23–29	
Proverbs 5:1–6	
Proverbs 6:24–26	

* What types of problems result from adultery today?

* Brainstorm ways of promoting chastity and protecting marriage.

5. What virtue is described in the following passages?

Ecclesiastes 8:1–9	
1 Samuel 15:22	
Proverbs 19:16	
Sirach 3:6	

* In what areas of life do you find stubbornness rather than obedience (deadlines, speed limits, staying within the budget, etc.)? How can you improve in obedience?

6. Find a common sentiment in these passages.

Ecclesiastes 8:10–17	
Romans 11:33–34	

* What can you do when you find God's ways inscrutable or troubling?

7. Identify the advice Qoheleth gives in these passages.

Ecclesiastes 8:15	
Ecclesiastes 9:7	
Ecclesiastes 11:9	

8. How and with whom should someone be enjoying life?

Ecclesiastes 9:9	
Malachi 2:14–16	

9. Explain the drama in Ecclesiastes 9:13–18.

* Has there been a time when you didn't get credit for the good you did?

10. Find some warnings in these verses.

Ecclesiastes 10:8	
Proverbs 26:27	
Sirach 27:29	

11. What can you learn from these verses?

Ecclesiastes 10:12	
Sirach 21:18–21	

12. Put Ecclesiastes 11:1 into your own words. Have you ever tried this?

13. How can you prevent your words from sounding foolish?

Psalm 141:3	
Sirach 22:27	

* What practical things do you do to control your tongue?

14. What are two main ideas of Ecclesiastes 11:1–6?

* Explain a practical application for Ecclesiastes 11:1.

15. What instruction is given in Ecclesiastes 11:9?

* Explain a practical way that you could apply Ecclesiastes 11:9 to your life.

16. Find some wise advice from Ecclesiastes 11:10.

* Put Ecclesiastes 11:10 into your words and give a practical application of it.

17. When should you think about God? Ecclesiastes 12:1–7

18. List some of the Preacher's accomplishments.

* Now list some of your accomplishments. What has made you proud?

19. What is Qoheleth's final piece of advice? Ecclesiastes 12:13

20. Ultimately, what will God do? Ecclesiastes 12:14

* What is the best piece of advice you could give to a younger person?

Chapter 13

Song of Songs
Song of Solomon 1–4

My beloved speaks and says to me:
"Arise, my love, my dove, my fair one,
and come away;"
Song of Solomon 2:10

Out of Place? — The presence of the Song of Solomon, also called the Song of Songs, or Canticle of Canticles in the Old Testament, is puzzling. Why is there a book in the Bible without any apparent religious theme or moral lesson, and in which God is never mentioned? No mention is made of any of the major topics of the Old Testament, like election, covenant, prophecy, exile, conversion, or salvation. The only interest of the book seems to be to describe in unabashed detail the love between a woman and a man. There is probably no other book in Scripture that has been so diversely interpreted as the Song of Songs. Its interpretations range from profound mysticism to profane love poetry. A good way to appreciate and understand why the Song of Solomon has a place in the Bible is to realize what the Bible is.

Talking about God — It is God who speaks in the Bible. The word of human authors is inspired. Through the work of the Holy Spirit, Sacred Scripture truly is the word *of* God. But there is more to it. The Bible also speaks *about* God; it is theo–logy or God–talk. In general, it is not easy to speak about God in a manner that does justice to Him, for all our words are derived from our limited human experience. In the Bible there are various ways in which God is spoken about. Sometimes completely new words have been created, like *r'chamim,* which denotes the love that is unique to God and which is often translated as "mercy."

A very frequent biblical mode of speech about God is the use of symbols and metaphors. In a way, all language consists of symbols, in the sense that a word is never the thing itself, which it denotes. Symbols are constructs which point to something else. Metaphors compare two or more things through association without the use of "as" or "like" as in a simile. Of all the symbols that human life has to offer, two symbols have a special importance in the Bible: (1) covenant, and (2) marriage. These concepts are derived from human experience, but can serve to point beyond the human sphere to God.

Covenant — The concept of covenant arises from the political scene. In the ancient Middle East, rulers made treaties with their subjected neighbors. Such treaties stated agreements about military support and payments to be made. "Covenant" is a term used profusely in the Bible to speak symbolically about God, allowing the biblical authors to highlight various aspects of the relationship between God and His people. A typical expression of this covenantal relationship is found in Exodus: *"and I will take you for* *my people, and I will be your God; and you shall know that I am the* LORD *your God, who has brought you out from under the burdens of the Egyptians"* (Exodus 6:7). This covenant requires the people to live up to their part of it, as the prophets never tire of repeating, *"Obey my voice, and I will be your God, and you shall be my people; and walk in all the way that I command you, that it may be well with you"* (Jeremiah 7:23; see also Jeremiah 11:3–4 and Ezekiel 36:28). The Ten Commandments are the most succinct formulation of the people's side of the covenant.

Marriage — The reality of marriage arises from the scene of daily domestic life. The prophets of the Old Testament have especially applied marriage as a symbol of God's relationship to His people. Their message is not always easily grasped. While marriage is known to people of all times and places, it is also conditioned by time and culture, and often distorted. Marriage is a reality that embraces many aspects, nearly all of which have been used by the biblical authors to speak about God: falling and being in love, longing for the beloved, marriage, fidelity, reconciliation, and fertility. Marriage is also a very rich symbol in the sense that it can be applied in many contexts. In several wisdom books, Wisdom personified is a woman and the relationship of the seeker of wisdom to Lady Wisdom is described in terms of searching and longing for her. The marriage symbol reaches its full potential in the New Testament when applied to the Messiah and His bride, the Church. It is against the backdrop of the symbolic language of prophets and wisdom books that the presence of the Song of Songs in the Bible can be understood.

Allegory — In the Jewish tradition, the love poem has long been read as an *historical* allegory. An allegory is a kind of protracted metaphor. In the case of the Song of Songs, the woman represents the people in a particular historical situation, while her lover is identified with God. Thus the verse *My beloved speaks and says to me: "Arise, my love, my dove, my fair one, and come away"* (Song of Solomon 2:10) is understood as God addressing the people in servitude in Egypt and calling them to go out of slavery to the promised land. Reading the Song of Solomon as historical allegory was intended to give the faithful some insight into the mighty deeds of God in history on behalf of His people.

Sometimes this poem was read as a *mystical* allegory, in which the two lovers are interpreted as the soul of the believer and God. In fact, this way of reading secured the place of the Song of Songs in the canon in the difficult times at the end of the first century AD. The destruction of the Temple in AD 70 by the Romans, and the strict prohibition for Jews not to set foot in Jerusalem, necessitated a redefinition of Judaism. This resulted in an energetic debate within Judaism about which books should be part of the canon. The mystical interpretation of Rabbi Akiba, a famous Jewish mystic, was largely responsible for the fact that the Song of Songs maintained its position in the Hebrew canon. Mystical allegory has been the main method of interpretation of this Book of wisdom literature in the Christian tradition until the eighteenth century AD.

Origin — With only eight chapters, the Song of Solomon is relatively short. It is more of a lengthy poem than a book. It is not known with certainty when and by whom the poem was written. Some parts of it may date back to the time of King Solomon. The fact that the cities of Tirza and Jerusalem are mentioned together (Song of Solomon 6:4) seems to point to a period when the land was still unified. Only after the reign of Solomon was the kingdom divided into a Northern Kingdom, Israel, with Tirza as capital (during the reign of Omri, Samaria became the capital of the North), and a Southern Kingdom, Judah, with Jerusalem as its capital. Sometimes the wealth and riches of Jerusalem are taken as evidence of its historical origin. The books of Samuel and Kings mention that there was much splendor and wealth in Jerusalem during the day of Solomon, but since this richness was legendary, the description of the city in the Song of Songs is not conclusive to a certain date.

The presence of a Persian loanword in Song of Solomon 4:12 (*pardes*=garden of enjoyment, paradise) makes it probable that the poem was re-written after the return from the Babylonian exile around 539 BC. In its final form, the poem might even be dated much later, since it also contains loanwords from Greek, such as *appirjon* meaning "palanquin or carriage" (Song of Solomon 3:9). Greek was used in Palestine from the third century BC onward, but was more widely used in the latter half of the second century BC and in the first century BC.

Irrespective of its origin or original context, this love poem has been incorporated into Sacred Scripture, and the reason seems to be that it was recognized as a symbol for the relationship between God and His people, and between Lady Wisdom and the seeker of wisdom. Prophets like Jeremiah, Hosea, and Isaiah, as well as certain wisdom passages, such as Proverbs 1:20–28; 9:1–6; Sirach 4:11–19; 6:23–31; 51:13–22, provided the context in which such recognition could take place. The fact that the title mentions Solomon serves not an historical but rather an interpretive function. King Solomon is traditionally known as the patron of wisdom (1 Kings 5:12). Thus the entire book is characterized as wisdom literature. The same effect is achieved by the conclusion of the poem, in which the last verses bear a strong resemblance to wisdom texts. There is a proverb in Song of Solomon 8:6–7 and two short parables in Song of Solomon 8:8–10, 11–12.

Name — The beauty of this love poetry is undeniable and is hinted at by the name Song of Songs, or Canticle of Canticles, which expresses the superlative, meaning the most wonderful of songs. "King of Kings" denotes the greatest of all kings (Ezra 7:12; Ezekiel 26:7; Daniel 2:37; 2 Maccabees 13:4; 1 Timothy 6:15; Revelation 17:14; 19:16). "Lord of lords" proclaims the Most High Lord (Deuteronomy 10:17; Psalm 136:3; 1 Timothy 6:15; Revelation 17:14; 19:16).

Song of Songs may seem an odd title for a book, but in fact, as is the case with many books of the Old Testament, it has no separate title, but its first words serve as the title. In tradition, several biblical books received more descriptive titles. The book known to us as Genesis is actually called *bere'shith* in Hebrew or "in the beginning" after its opening words. The book commonly known as Exodus is called *w'elleh shemot* in

Hebrew for "these are the names." The title "Song of Songs" was commonly accepted as its opening Hebrew words.

The Characters — The shape of the love poem is intriguing. Two young people express their longing and love for each other in delightful imagery and metaphors, and the perspective constantly shifts between the two of them. They enjoy each other's company and are captivated by the beauty of the other, and therefore suffer in not being together or being able to come together. There is a slight imbalance in the role of the characters and the main perspective appears to be that of the woman. The poem uses more words to describe her thoughts and emotions than his, and at the same time, it also seems to pay homage to this woman in love. This fluctuation of perspectives is characteristic of the Song of Songs. It provides a first clue for understanding the structure of the poem.

The fact that often the lovers in their longing for each other imagine what the other would say if he or she were present makes it difficult to follow the shifts in perspective. Thus, the woman in conveying her longing for her beloved imagines what he would say and speaks for him (Song of Solomon 2:10b–15). This is a powerful illustration of the depth of longing each person has for the other. A mirroring dynamic is found on various levels. For example, the poem opens with the woman longing for the beloved's kisses, comparing them with sweet wine and fragrance. Later in Song of Solomon 4:10–11, this is perfectly mirrored by the beloved who longs for her kisses using the same metaphors of wine and fragrant oils. Ultimately, this dynamic of longing is a profound expression of the nature of love from the beginning of creation (Genesis 2:23).

Apart from the opening and conclusion, in which there is a vivid mixture of various voices, there is a fairly clear dialogue between the woman in love and her beloved. There is a series of songs by the woman about her beloved, and to these correspond songs by the beloved. Oddly, in the middle of the dialogue there is a voice that belongs to neither and is usually attributed to a choir. The flow of the dialogue thus yields a first idea of the organization of the poem:

Prologue		Song 1:1–2:5
	Woman	Song 2:8–15 + 3:1–4
Choir		Song 3:6–11
	Beloved	Song 4:1–7 + 4:8–5:1
Choir		Song 5:9
	Woman	Song 5:2–8 + 5:10–16
	Beloved	Song 6:4–12 + 7:1–9
	Woman	Song 7:10–14 + 8:1–4
Epilogue		Song 8:5–14

Repetitions — Repetition is, by definition, a formal element of speech. In poetry, it often serves the purpose of structuring the text, and therefore a good way to understand the Song of Songs as a whole is to focus on what is repeated. The author makes use of various types of repetition. Sometimes whole lines are repeated verbatim. *I adjure you, O daughters of Jerusalem, by the gazelles or the deer of the field, that you stir not up nor awaken love until it please* (Song of Solomon 2:7; 3:5; 8:4). Sometimes, short expressions and clusters of words recur: *I am sick with love* (Song of Solomon 2:5; 5:8), or *among the lilies* (Song of Solomon 2:16; 4:5; 6:3). The complexity of the phenomenon of repetition can be seen in the following *chiasme*, which is repetition in reversed order.

Song of Solomon 3:6—4:5	Song of Solomon 6:4–10
What is that? (Song of Solomon 3:6)	*Who is this?* (Song of Solomon 6:10)
Sixty heroes (Song of Solomon 3:7)	*Sixty queens* (Song of Solomon 6:8)
Beauty (Song of Solomon 4:1–5)	*Beauty* (Song of Solomon 6:4–7)

An overview of all kinds of repetitions and their respective function and location in the Song of Songs helps to understand the basic structure of the poem. Most of the repetitions refer somehow to the coming and staying together of the two lovers. The point where the repetitive themes begin to be repeated appears to be between Song of Solomon 5:1 and 5:2, which corresponds more or less to the center of the poem. Without having a strict symmetry, in these parts of the poem there is a movement from an initial separation and longing toward a final reunion.

Theme	Part I	Part II
Being separate, he longs for her.	Song 2:8–17	Song 5:2–5
She longs for him.	Song 3:1–5	Song 5:6–6:3
They face each other in admiration and desire.	Song 4:1–6	Song 6:4–7:9
They come together.	Song 4:8–5:1	Song 7:10–8:4

The movement from being separate to being together is a main structural idea of the poem and is found in the prologue. The woman dreams about being introduced into the presence of the king, and ultimately her longing is realized (Song of Solomon 1:4; 2:4). The recurrence of entire verses appears to have a formal function. They serve as transitions between sections of the poem. On the basis of the various types of repetition, the shift of characters and the movement from separation to being united, one can approximate the structure of the poem.

Song of Solomon, Song of Songs, or Canticle of Canticles			
PROLOGUE		Song 1:1 – 2:5	*[Mention of friends, 1:7]* Concluded with repeated verses in Song 2:6–7
PART I	Bride	Song 2:8–17	Longing for the beloved Concluded with repeated verses in Song 2:16–17
	Bride	Song 3:1–4	Longing for the beloved Concluded with repeated verse in Song 3:5 *[Choir – Song 3:6–11]*
	Bridegroom	Song 4:1–5	Facing each other Concluded with repeated verse in Song 4:6
	Bridegroom	Song 4:7 – 5:1	Being together *[Invitation to friends, 5:1]*
PART II	Bride	Song 5:2–7	Longing for the beloved Concluded with repeated verse in Song 5:8 *[Choir – Song 5:9]*
	Bride	Song 5:10–16	Longing for the beloved *[Choir – Song 6:1]* Concluded with repeated verses in Song 6:2–3
	Bridegroom	Song 6:4–12	Facing each other *[Choir – Song 6:13]*
	Bridegroom	Song 7:1–9	Facing each other
	Bride	Song 7:10–14	Being together
	Bride	Song 8:1–4	Being together Concluded with repeated verses in Song 8:3–4
EPILOGUE		Song 8:5–14	*[Mention of friends, 8:13]*

1. Read the Song of Songs in one sitting, and write your favorite verse.

2. The love of the beloved is better than what? Song of Solomon 1:2–4

3. What is the cause of the woman's darkness? Song of Solomon 1:6–7

4. What is the occupation of the bridegroom? Song of Solomon 1:7

5. How does the bridegroom describe the bride's beauty? Song of Solomon 1:9–11

6. What does the Psalmist seek to behold? Psalm 27:4

7. How does the Psalmist describe God's love? Psalm 63:1–9

8. What is the most perfect example of love? John 15:12–13

* Describe the most perfect example of human love you have witnessed.

9. Where is the beloved taken? Song of Solomon 2:4

10. What admonition is given in Song of Solomon 2:7 and 3:5?

* Paraphrase the above admonition for young lovers today.

** What problems can occur when love is awakened before its time?

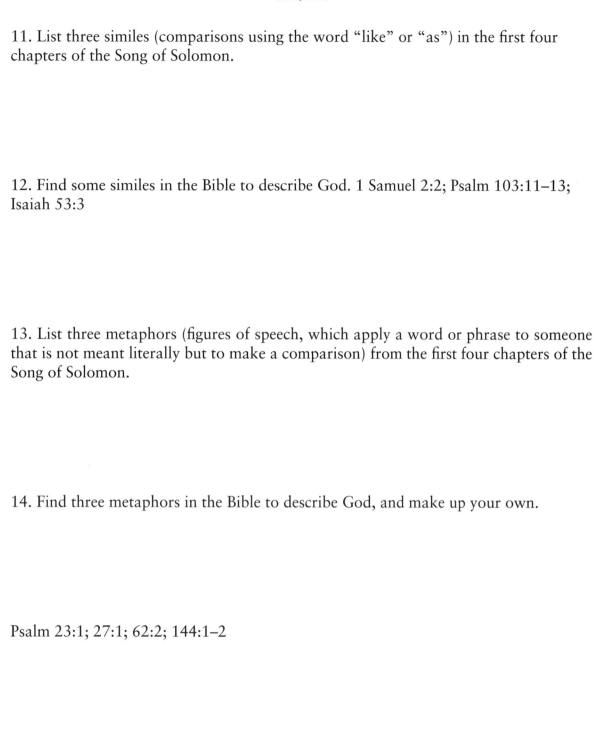

11. List three similes (comparisons using the word "like" or "as") in the first four chapters of the Song of Solomon.

12. Find some similes in the Bible to describe God. 1 Samuel 2:2; Psalm 103:11–13; Isaiah 53:3

13. List three metaphors (figures of speech, which apply a word or phrase to someone that is not meant literally but to make a comparison) from the first four chapters of the Song of Solomon.

14. Find three metaphors in the Bible to describe God, and make up your own.

Psalm 23:1; 27:1; 62:2; 144:1–2

15. Describe the personification repeated in Song of Solomon 2:17 and 4:6.

16. Identify the activities desired in the following verses.

Song of Solomon 2:17	
Song of Solomon 4:5–6	
Song of Solomon 8:14	

17. What activity is repeated in the following verses?

Song of Solomon 2:16	
Song of Solomon 6:3	
Song of Solomon 7:10	

18. What affliction do these verses describe? Song of Solomon 2:5 and 5:8

* Have you ever been lovesick?

19. What do the following passages encourage you to do?

Psalm 27:8	
Song of Solomon 3:2	
Isaiah 55:6	

20. Who alone could meet the description in Song of Solomon 4:7?

Chapter 14

The Context of Love
Song of Solomon 5–8

Set me as a seal upon your heart,
as a seal upon your arm;
for love is strong as death
Song of Solomon 8:6

The Bride — The main character of the Song of Songs is the woman in love. She has no name and about her nothing historical is known with any certainty, but her point of view is the dominant perspective of the poem. The mention of King Solomon in verse one has led some to think of a queen, perhaps the African Queen of Sheba, especially as she professes to be *very dark, but comely* (Song of Solomon 1:5). The text clearly indicates that she is an Israelite girl *scorched by the sun* (Song of Solomon 1:6). "Dark" should be understood hyperbolically, and not indicative of race, for the general ideal of beauty in the Ancient Near East associated fair skin with beauty. The beauty of the bridegroom is described as *all radiant and ruddy* (Song of Solomon 5:10), whereas the beauty of the bride is described as *fair as the moon, bright as the sun* (Song of Solomon 6:10). The daughters of Jerusalem probably reflect this description, and repeatedly the bride, as if looking in a mirror, compares herself to them, as if seeking their approval.

New Testament authors have re-read the poem through the lens of the life, death, and Resurrection of Jesus. Especially in the fourth gospel, the evangelist reveals what the appropriate attitude toward Jesus is with the help of the woman in love from the Song of Songs. She proves to be a model for the disciples.

John describes the first encounter between Jesus and one of His followers, Mary Magdalene, after the Resurrection. The whole passage follows the rhythm and themes of the woman in love searching for her beloved: darkness, looking, not finding, asking, turning around, finding, holding on to, not letting go.

Song of Songs	The Gospel of John
*Upon my bed by **night** I sought him whom my soul loves; I sought him but found him not.* ***I sought him but found him not.*** Song of Solomon 3:1–2	*Mary Magdalene came to the tomb early, **while it was still dark** …* *They have taken the Lord out of the tomb, and **we do not know where they have laid him.*** John 20:1–2

Song of Songs	The Gospel of John
*The **watchmen** found me, as they went about in the city.* Song of Solomon 3:3	*She saw **two angels in white**, sitting where the body of Jesus had lain,* John 20:12
*"**Have you seen him** whom my soul loves?"* Song of Solomon 3:3	*"They have taken away my Lord, and **I do not know where** they have laid him"* John 20:13
*Scarcely had I **passed them**, when I **found him** whom my soul loves.* Song of Solomon 3:4	*Saying this, she **turned round** and saw **Jesus standing*** John 20:14
***I held him** and would not let him go ...* Song of Solomon 3:4	*Jesus said to her, "**Do not hold me**"* John 20:17
*...until I had brought him into **my mother's house**, and into the chamber of her that conceived me.* Song of Solomon 3:4	*..."for I have not yet **ascended to the Father**; but go to my brethren and say to them, I am ascending to my Father and your Father, to my God and your God."* John 20:17

The same sequence with the same elements—seeking, turning around, asking, the Rabboni, finding—is also found, more succinctly, in the first encounter of Jesus with his disciples in John 1:35–39. In both instances, the bride in the Song of Songs provides the model which the evangelist uses to inculcate that the disciples have to seek Jesus and long for Him with the longing of a bride, and that they, both in their first encounter and after the Resurrection, have to turn to Him and learn from Him as Teacher. Jesus Himself reveals who He is and how He is found. Especially in John 20, it is evident that the Song of Songs forms a matrix providing the elements with which the encounter is described.

The Resurrection scene takes place in a garden, and Mary Magdalene, looking for where the body was *lying*, first thought the *standing* Jesus to be a gardener. The Song of Songs is also situated in a garden, and at times the bride herself is likened to a vineyard and a closed garden (Song of Solomon 1:6; 5:1; 8:12). Furthermore, the evangelist knows that there were more women at the tomb, but concentrates all attention to just one of them, Mary of Magdala, because this focus allows a closer comparison with the bride from the

Song of Songs, and thus allows a better understanding of what the Resurrection really means. In light of the Song of Songs, the second part of the encounter, after the initial recognition, becomes clearer. John modifies the pattern of the Song of Songs to stress an important point, which is clarified in different ways in other gospels. The meaning of Christ's Resurrection is learned not just by an apparition of the Risen Lord, but also by His teaching. The life of the Risen Jesus is not like the life one receives from an earthly mother, but His Risen life is absolutely new and comes from His Heavenly Father. Similarly, the disciples on the way to Emmaus see the Risen Lord but do not recognize Him, until He teaches them what is written in Scripture about Him (Luke 24:13–35).

The Bridegroom — Many have tried to identify King Solomon as the author of the Song of Songs. Solomon, however, never speaks in the first person singular, but is nearly always referred to in the third person. The references to the beloved (Song of Solomon 1:5; 3:7–11; 8:11) nearly always use the third person, and never purport to indicate Solomon as author. Rather, the wisdom literature plays on Solomon's reputation as the patron of wisdom. Since one thousand songs and three thousand proverbs are ascribed to Solomon (1 Kings 4:32), they provide a key for interpreting the Song of Songs as a wisdom text written in the style of Solomon.

The beloved is mostly portrayed as a shepherd, and the woman in love wants to know where he pastures his flock. Nevertheless, thrice he is called *king* (Song of Solomon 1:4; 1:12; 7:5). Here the point of reference is not Solomon, but any Davidic king whose wedding was of national importance. Psalm 45 describes such a royal wedding and indicates why it was so important. Royal offspring are essential to ensure the divine promise to David (Psalm 45:16). In short, in the Old Testament the king from the house of David is the bridegroom par excellence.

New Testament authors and the Fathers of the Church make use of the role of the beloved king to proclaim Jesus. In the fourth gospel after the raising of Lazarus, Jesus is anointed in the house of Lazarus, Martha, and Mary (John 12:1–8). This anointing is described with words and imagery taken from the Song of Songs (Song of Solomon 1:12; 8:7b). Like the king in the Song of Songs, Jesus is reclining at table while Mary anoints His feet with pure nard, and the whole house is filled with its fragrance. This stark contrast with the stench of death at the tomb of Lazarus (John 11:39) demonstrates Jesus' victory over death. When Judas protests the costliness of the nard being wasted, Jesus rebukes him for trying to put a price on love, reminiscent of Song of Songs 8:7b.

The King — The lengthiest passage about the king is found in Song of Solomon 3:6–11. It is special in that it does not have nature, a garden, or a rural setting for its scene, but rather a city and a royal ambience. It opens with watchmen posted high on the city wall (Isaiah 62:6), noticing a cloud of dust on the horizon and announcing the arrival of a group. The dust cloud is immediately transformed into a cloud of fragrance and frankincense. It is the royal entourage of the king approaching the city for his wedding. The carriage is described in great detail: the royal throne is made of wood and is *lovingly wrought within,* or *fitted with love* (Song of Solomon 3:10). The Greek translation shows that the word "love" was depicted in a kind of mosaic on the back of the seat, employing the rare word *lithostrotos* meaning "inlay of stone." Sitting on this throne of love, the king wears his wedding crown (Isaiah 61:10). John evokes this scene, using the same rare word *lithostrotos* when Jesus stands before Pilate (John 19:13), wearing his crown of thorns, robed in royal purple. John identifies Jesus as the bridegroom king, who is motivated by love.

Voice of the Bridegroom — John Chapter 3 provides a beautiful example of how the Song of Songs gains deeper significance in the New Testament. Jesus is baptizing in Judea and His disciples are with Him. John the Baptist is also baptizing (John 3:22–23). The other gospels do not include this information. Later, John the evangelist surprisingly corrects himself and says that Jesus did not baptize (John 4:1–2). Why would he say this in the first place, knowing it was not so? This information serves to explain how confusion can arise: where to go for baptism? Who baptizes better? There is then an *understandable* controversy between a seeker and a follower of the Baptist. The disciples of John are zealous for their master and ask him to intervene. John the Baptist takes this opportunity to give his final testimony in the Bible. John's testimony comes in the form of some riddles: "*He who has the bride is the bridegroom,*" and "*The friend of the bridegroom … rejoices at the bridegroom's voice*" (John 3:29).

This phrase is not an invention of John the Baptist, nor of John the Evangelist. It is the language of the Old Testament, specifically that of the prophets and the Song of Songs. With a catchy rhyme, Jeremiah announces doom and subsequent salvation: *you shall not hear the voice of mirth and the voice of gladness, the voice of the bridegroom and the voice of the bride* (Jeremiah 16:9; 25:10; 33:10–11; Revelation 18:21–24). This prophetic expression derives from a universal fact—marriage is the God–given key of life. Not hearing the voices of the bridegroom and bride signals the epitome of society's doom. No marriages mean there will be no children, and thus society will die. There would be no future generations, if marriage and childbearing cease. In contrast, hearing the voice of the bridegroom announces redemption and life. It means the Messiah has come.

John the Baptist speaks of Jesus as the bridegroom in an indirect way by referring to himself as the best man, the friend who finds ultimate joy when he hears the voice of the bridegroom. Drawing on hints in the New Testament of preparations that the bride of the Messiah must undergo (see Ephesians 5:26; 2 Corinthians 11:2; Revelation 21:2), it seems, as some Fathers of the Church propose, that John the Baptist understood himself as the one who prepares the bride by cleansing her in a baptism of repentance. This is not what John's followers had in mind, but the Baptist leaves no room for misunderstanding here. He borrows again from the Song of Songs—a book that consists practically entirely of the voices of a bridegroom and a bride—the expressions *he who has the bride,* and *the friend [of the groom]* (Song of Solomon 2:16a; John 3:29).

Context of Love — Why would the final testimony of John the Baptist (John 3:22–30) be "inserted" into the nightly conversation of Jesus with Nicodemus (John 3:1–21, 31–36)? The essence of the witness of the Baptist consists in the novelty that it is the Messiah who has come as bridegroom. In the prophetic books, the role of the bridegroom has been reserved for God. God loves His bride, His people: that is what the Old Testament proclaims. *As the bridegroom rejoices over the bride, so shall your God rejoice over you* (Isaiah 62:5). What is new in the New Testament, and what Jesus therefore explains to Nicodemus, is that God, in fact, *so loved the world that he gave his only-begotten Son* (John 3:16). The overwhelming love of God reveals the *heavenly things* (John 3:12) that only the Son of man can speak about, because He is the only one to have descended from heaven. The Son of man embodies the full extent of God's love and He will demonstrate His love *to the end* (John 13:1) when He is lifted up, just as Moses lifted up the serpent. In both cases, the people who look up in faith are saved. The nightly conversation is indeed the right context for the evangelist to reveal Jesus as the bridegroom and to explain the context of God's unfathomable love.

God's passionate love for his people—for humanity—is at the same time a forgiving love. It is so great that it turns God against himself, his love against his justice. Here Christians can see a dim prefigurement of the mystery of the Cross: so great is God's love for man that by becoming man he follows him even into death, and so reconciles justice and love.

The philosophical dimension to be noted in this biblical vision, and its importance from the standpoint of the history of religions, lies in the fact that on the one hand we find ourselves before a strictly metaphysical image of God: God is the absolute and ultimate source of all being; but this universal principle of creation—the *Logos*, primordial reason—is at the same time a lover with all the passion of a true love. *Eros* is thus supremely ennobled, yet at the same time it is so purified as to become one with *agape*. We can thus see how the reception of the *Song of Songs* in the canon of Sacred Scripture was soon explained by the idea that these love songs ultimately describe God's relation to man and man's relation to God. Thus the *Song of Songs* became, both in Christian and Jewish literature, a source of mystical knowledge and experience, an expression of the essence of biblical faith: that man can indeed enter into union with God—his primordial aspiration. But this union is no mere fusion, a sinking in the nameless ocean of the Divine; it is a unity which creates love, a unity in which both God and man remain themselves and yet become fully one. As Saint Paul says: *He who is united to the Lord becomes one spirit with him* (1 Corinthians 6:17).

Pope Benedict XVI, *Deus Caritas Est "God Is Love"*
(December 25, 2005), 10

1. Read the Song of Solomon in a different translation of Scripture from the one you read last week, and write your favorite verse.

2. Identify the repetitive claims of mutual belonging in the following verses.

Song of Solomon 2:16	
Song of Solomon 6:3	
Song of Solomon 7:10–11	

3. List some ways that human beings can meet their needs for belonging.

4. How can you seek the love of your soul?

Song of Solomon 1:7–8	
Song of Solomon 3:1–4	
Psalm 62:1–5	
Psalm 73:25–28	
CCC 2709	

5. Find the repetitive phrase describing *a location* in the following verses.

Song of Solomon 2:16	
Song of Solomon 4:5	
Song of Solomon 6:3	

* Describe some special locations in which you feel close to your loved ones.

** Is there a special place in which you feel especially close to the Lord?

6. What natural phenomenon is described in Song of Solomon 8:5b?

* You might find different understandings from different translations used by members of your small group. Father Jan will clarify in the lecture video.

7. Find some similes, which use "like" or "as" in the following verses.

Song of Solomon 5:12	
Song of Solomon 5:13	
Song of Solomon 6:5–7	
Song of Solomon 7:3–10	

* Write a simile to describe God, the beloved.

8. Find some metaphors from the following verses.

Song of Solomon 5:11	
Song of Solomon 5:13–15	
Song of Solomon 7:2	
Song of Solomon 7:4b	
Song of Solomon 8:9	

* Write a metaphor for the Lord, your beloved.

9. What unique expression of "human love" is described in these verses?

Song of Solomon 7:10–13	
CCC 1611	
CCC 1604	

10. What married couple do you know who best exemplifies God's love?

11. Find a comparison from the following verses.

Song of Solomon 3:7	
Song of Solomon 6:8	

12. What physical characteristic is described in these passages?

Song of Solomon 4:1–5	
Song of Solomon 6:4–7	

13. How important is physical beauty to you? Use scripture to explain.

14. Find some reluctance and the result in Song of Solomon 5:2–6.

15. What did the watchmen do? Song of Solomon 5:7

16. Where can you find perfection and flawlessness?

Song of Solomon 6:9	
Matthew 5:44–45, 48	
1 John 4:16–18	

17. How and in whom should you look for perfect love? CCC 2745

18. What is strong as death? Song of Solomon 8:6

19. When will we see love stronger than death? CCC 1040

20. What can you learn from the Song of Solomon 8:7, and John 12:4–7?

CHAPTER 15

Wisdom and Justice
Wisdom 1–6:21

The beginning of wisdom is the most sincere desire for instruction,
and concern for instruction is love of her,
and love of her is the keeping of her laws,
and giving heed to her laws is assurance of immortality,
and immortality brings one near to God,
so the desire for wisdom leads to a kingdom.
Wisdom 6:17–20

In order to attain wisdom, one must desire it, ask God for wisdom and live righteously, in obedience to God's Law. Imagine a young person leaving home and traveling to a large, cosmopolitan city where he encounters many new and fascinating ideas. Soon his faith is challenged as he mingles with the people and ideas around him. What could be done for someone in danger of losing his faith, or someone struggling to keep the faith in the midst of adversity and suffering? Perhaps this was the concern facing the author of *Sophia Salomonos,* Greek for "The Wisdom of Solomon." *Sophia* is Greek for "wisdom."

King Solomon lived ten centuries before this book was penned. But, an anonymous and learned Greek-speaking Jew used a literary device common in Old Testament times to attribute his writing to Solomon. Wisdom is the last book written in the Old Testament in the century preceding the birth of Jesus, around 15–50 BC. The author, a pious Jew with a vast knowledge of the Sacred Scripture and the Hellenistic philosophy, rhetoric, and culture, lived in Alexandria, Egypt. He wrote in excellent Greek. His purpose was to build up the faith of Jews living in the *diaspora* (Jews living outside the Holy Land), to defend the wisdom of the Law against pagan philosophies, and to call people back to their covenant with God.

Historical Background — The Roman general Pompey entered Jerusalem in 63 BC, killing over a thousand Jews in the temple area before forcing his way into the Holy of Holies, causing many Jews to flee to Egypt and elsewhere. On his return to Rome, Pompey established a triumvirate with Julius Caesar and Marcus Licinius Crassus. Pompey was assassinated in Egypt in 48 BC. Later, Marcus Brutus and Gaius Cassius assassinated Julius Caesar on the ides of March 44 BC.

Octavian, the great-nephew of Caesar, later formed a triumvirate with Mark Antony and Marcus Lepidus. Mark Antony married the sister of Octavian and then abandoned her. Antony and Cleopatra then presented themselves as Greek gods to the people. Ultimately they committed suicide in Egypt. In 27 BC, the senate in Rome gave Octavian the title "Caesar Augustus." He ruled from 27 BC to 14 AD and made Egypt a province of the Roman Empire. During this time, Herod the Great ruled in Judea (37 BC–AD 4). Herod ruthlessly murdered anyone who provoked his paranoid suspicions, including his wife, his mother-in-law, two sons, and the high priest. It was in this volatile political climate that the Book of Wisdom was written.

Diaspora Jews in Alexandria — At this time Alexandria, Egypt, housed the largest Jewish population of any city in the diaspora. Alexandria had many synagogues and one Great Synagogue. A city of a million inhabitants, Alexandria was on the Mediterranean Sea west of the Nile Delta, a prime port and junction of east and west in the ancient world. It was a commercial hub and a center of scholarly activity. Greek philosophy, drama, literature, rhetoric, mathematics, and science attracted the finest minds of the time.

Alexandria was the primary center of Hellenistic Judaism by the first century BC. It is in this place that, since about 250 BC, biblical scholars were translating the Hebrew Scriptures into Greek, creating what would become known as the Septuagint. About this time, a brilliant scholar, Philo of Alexandria (20 BC – AD 50), would try to synthesize Hebrew revelation and Greek philosophy. Some time before the birth of Philo, another Jewish scholar wrote this last Book of the Old Testament. Standing alongside the tradition of Jesus Ben Sira, this author was a preacher who showed how revelation illuminates understanding to provide a truthful view of reality. Intellectual Jews, as well as many other people for centuries beyond, would be blessed by his writing.

Exhortation to love justice — The Book of Wisdom begins with three exhortations, three verbs—love, think, and seek. To love the Lord with uprightness (Wisdom 1:1) implies the need to pray. The scripture exhorts the faithful to love God in prayer and worship. To think of the Lord with uprightness (Wisdom 1:1) means to obey God's commands, to act justly, and to avoid evil. Finally, one must seek God's wisdom in His Word and His Law.

Wisdom is an attribute of God, and the gift of God. In the Old Testament, wisdom is personified as a woman (Proverbs 1:20–23; 8:1–36; 9:1–6; Baruch 3:9–4:4; Sirach 24:1–21). Wisdom is a characteristic of God, not a separate being, and not synonymous with God. In these passages, wisdom is closely linked with the Spirit of the Lord. *Wisdom is a kindly spirit* (Wisdom 1:6). *The Spirit of the Lord has filled the world, and that which holds all things together knows what is said* (Wisdom 1:7) is a familiar text from the Roman Catholic liturgy on Pentecost.

Immortality is the ultimate reward of righteousness. God did not make death, rather the devil brought death into the world. The Wisdom author identifies the serpent in the Garden of Eden as the devil, the source of death (Genesis 3:1–24, Wisdom 2:24). The concept of immortality was only gradually being revealed to the Chosen People. Although they did not enjoy the full Christian understanding of the concept of the resurrection of the body, at least the hope of an afterlife for the just souls emerges here. The same understanding is also expressed in Daniel and 2 Maccabees (Wisdom 3:1–9; 4:7–19; 5:15–16; Daniel 12:1–2; 2 Maccabees 7:11, 7:23, 7:36). Only God, who has power over life and death, can give the gift of immortality (Wisdom 2:23; 3:1–4; 4:1; 16:13). Eternal life will be the reward of the wise and righteous who die in the hope of living with God forever, in contrast to the foolish and wicked who expect nothing, and live as if there is no hereafter (Wisdom 2:5).

In ancient times and even today, people believe that God blesses the righteous with long life, children, health, and prosperity. In contrast, suffering (Wisdom 3:1–12), childlessness (Wisdom 3:13–4:6), and early death (Wisdom 4:7–19) were seen as signs of God's disfavor or punishment. Both the just and the wicked suffer, but the righteous embrace suffering and triumph in their trials. In dying, the just man, even though he dies prematurely can hope to arrive at a place of blessedness in the hand of God (Wisdom 3:1–4). And while children are always seen as blessings from God (Leviticus 26:9: Deuteronomy 7:14; 28:4; Psalm 128:1–4), there can also be a spiritual fruitfulness even for the barren. Childlessness with virtue is better than the prolific brood of the ungodly (Wisdom 4:1–3).

Virtuous people seek wisdom. The just see children as a gift from the Lord and beseech Him for godly offspring. The good name and memory of parents survive through their children (Sirach 40:19; Ruth 4:14). When there are no children, the hope of being remembered in one's offspring is lost (Job 18:17–19). For women especially, sterility can be a source of sorrow and humiliation. But, accepting God's will and embracing the trials of life can reap eternal blessings and rewards.

The picture of the just in Wisdom 3 is familiar, because it is the first reading of the Mass for All Soul's Day, November 2nd and is often used in funeral liturgies. This image is also found in the Fourth Servant Song of Isaiah and in Psalm 22:8–21.

Wisdom 3:1–4	Isaiah 52:13–15
But the souls of the righteous are in the hand of God, and no torment will ever touch them. *In the eyes of the foolish they seemed to have died,* *and their departure was thought to be an affliction,* *and their going from us to be their destruction;* *but they are at peace.* *For though in the sight of men they were punished,* *their hope is full of immortality.*	*Behold, my servant shall prosper,* *he shall be exalted and lifted up,* *and shall be very high.* *As many were astonished at him – his appearance was so marred, beyond human semblance, and his form beyond that of the sons of men –* *so shall he startle many nations;* *kings shall shut their mouths because of him;* *for that which has not been told them they shall see, and that which they have not heard they shall understand.*

The foolishness of the wicked — The author contrasts the wisdom of the just with the foolishness of the evildoers. Given the political situation in Egypt, the readers of this book would have recently heard of the reversal of fortune of Antony and Cleopatra. One day they claimed they were gods and the next day they took their own lives. In that time, as in our own day, the wicked claim that "might makes right" (Wisdom 2:11) and that the weak are useless. But, the righteous one who fears God protects the weak, the poor, and the vulnerable (Exodus 22:21). God commands that mercy be shown to the poor and needy. Might does not always make right.

The paradox of the lives of the just and the unjust are shown in four sets of passages, called diptychs in Wisdom 3–4. Compare segments of these passages by looking at them side by side.

Just	Unjust
... the souls of the righteous are in the hand of God, and no torment will ever touch them ... because God tested them and found them worthy of himself (Wisdom 3:1, 3: 5)	*But the ungodly will be punished as their reasoning deserves, who disregarded the righteous man and rebelled against the Lord* (Wisdom 3:10)
... the fruit of good labors is renowned (Wisdom 3:15)	*... their old age will be without honor* (Wisdom 3:17)
... the memory of virtue is immortality, because it is known both by God and men (Wisdom 4:1)	*... their fruit will be useless...witnesses of evil against their parents when God examines them* (Wisdom 4:5–6)
But the righteous man, though he die early, will be at rest. ... for his soul was pleasing to the Lord (Wisdom 4:7, 4:14)	*They will come with dread when their sins are reckoned up, and their lawless deeds will convict them to their face.* (Wisdom 4:20)

These scriptures encourage each person to embrace wisdom and righteousness, and to shun foolishness and wickedness. Praying to God and obeying God's laws lay a foundation for virtue and wisdom. This last Book of the Old Testament was written just before the dawn of the Christian era, when God would reveal to people the just man, called Joseph (Matthew 1:19), who would be the foster father of the Just Man *par excellence*, Jesus Christ. The author of wisdom prepares the reader to recognize the One Just Man, Jesus of Nazareth, who would suffer and die early, not reaching advanced age.

The Early Church Fathers, including Saint Ambrose, identified Christ as the Wisdom of God. And Saint Paul described Christ as *the power of God and the wisdom of God* (1 Corinthians 1:24).

> "Teach me words rich in wisdom for you are Wisdom! Open my heart, you who have opened the Book! Open the door that is in Heaven, for you are the Door! If we are introduced through you, we will possess the eternal Kingdom. Whoever enters through you will not be deceived, for he cannot err who enters the dwelling place of Truth."
>
> (Saint Ambrose [AD 340–397] *Comment on Psalm 118, 9*)

1. According to Wisdom 1:1, what three things should you do?

2. Name some obstacles to obtaining wisdom. Wisdom 1:2–6

3. What happened in the following verses?

Wisdom 1:7	
Acts 2:4	

4. List some warnings from Wisdom 1:8–11.

5. What can you learn about death and how it came into the world?

CCC 391	
CCC 413	
Wisdom 1:13–14	
Wisdom 2:23–24	
CCC 1008	
CCC 1009	
CCC 2538	

6. What can you learn about immortality?

Wisdom 1:15	
Wisdom 2:23	
Wisdom 3:4	
Wisdom 5:15	
Wisdom 6:19	
CCC 366	

7. Since you will live forever, how should you now live? Romans 14:7–12

* If you were to give an account to God next week, what would you change now?

8. How do ungodly men think and behave?

Wisdom 1:16–2:3	
Wisdom 2:4–5	
Wisdom 2:6–11	
Wisdom 2:12–20	

9. Find some expressions indicating close ties between the just and the Lord.

Wisdom 2:13	
Wisdom 2:16	
Wisdom 2:18	

10. How were you created? Wisdom 2:23

11. Find some characteristics of the righteous and the ungodly.

Righteous	Wicked
Wisdom 3:1–9	Wisdom 3:10–12
Wisdom 3:13–15	Wisdom 3:16–19
Wisdom 4:1–2	Wisdom 4:3–6
Wisdom 4:7–16	Wisdom 4:17–20

12. What do Wisdom and Saint Thomas say about "spiritual maturity?"

Wisdom 4:7–9	
CCC 1308	

13. List three people you know who possess spiritual maturity.

* What could you do to grow in spiritual maturity?

14. Find examples of childlessness in the Bible. Genesis 17, 1 Samuel 1, Luke 1

15. Define "virtue." Wisdom 4:1, CCC 1803–1804. How can you grow in virtue?

16. How will the wicked ultimately be judged? Wisdom 4:20–5:23

17. What comfort can be found in Wisdom 6:6?

18. Who will be made holy? Wisdom 6:10

19. How can you attain wisdom? Wisdom 6:11–15

20. List three steps in obtaining wisdom. Wisdom 6:17–20

* What practical thing can you do this week to grow in wisdom?

Monthly Social Activity

This month, your small group will meet for coffee, tea, or a simple breakfast, lunch, or dessert in someone's home. Pray for this social event and for the host or hostess. Try, if at all possible, to attend.

After a short prayer and some time for small talk, reflect on the nature of wisdom. Think about the people you know who are wise and talk about one of them.

Example

◆ *My Dad has true wisdom. He loves God. He is content with his lot in life and expresses gratitude for all of his blessings. Everyone loves being around him. He makes everyone feel special and loved.*

Chapter 16

Praise of Wisdom
Wisdom 6:22–10:21

For wisdom, the fashioner of all things, taught me.
For in her there is a spirit that is intelligent, holy,
unique, manifold, subtle,
mobile, clear, unpolluted,
distinct, invulnerable, loving the good, keen,
irresistible, beneficent, humane,
steadfast, sure, free from anxiety,
all-powerful, overseeing all,
and penetrating through all spirits
that are intelligent and pure and most subtle.
Wisdom 7:22–23

The Nature of Wisdom — In this middle section of the Book of Wisdom, the author, identifying himself with Solomon, praises the essence and beauty of wisdom. After defining and describing wisdom, he reveals that from seeking wisdom and praying to God, the gift of wisdom was granted to him. Interestingly, in contrast to Antony and Cleopatra, who proclaimed to the people that they were gods with supernatural characteristics, Solomon, the wisest man to ever live, confesses that he is a mere *mortal, like all men* (Wisdom 7:1). For even kings have the same humble beginnings as all people on the earth. Solomon was born a baby—crying, being diapered, nursed— as all people are. Solomon shows that his wisdom is not the result of superhuman properties or god-like characteristics. Rather, he has wisdom because he prayed to God for wisdom. And God graciously answered his prayer and bestowed the gift of wisdom upon him.

Because Solomon had received such a great gift, he gave glory to God, the Giver of the gift. Solomon did not request wisdom for himself alone, but in order to be a wise king for others. Solomon did not hoard the magnificent gift of wisdom he had been given. His wisdom is excellent for those in leadership positions even today. Wisdom is essential for leaders in every age and time. Pray that God would grant wisdom to the leaders of peoples and nations today, as well. *A multitude of wise men is the salvation of the world, and a sensible king is the stability of his people. Therefore be instructed by my words, and you will profit* (Wisdom 6:24–25).

It would be difficult to find fault with this line of reasoning. Wisdom should be passed on from one generation to the next. And people should pray for wisdom for the leaders of nations. Foolish and selfish people in authority bring disaster, not only upon themselves, but also on the many innocent people who must suffer from their poor choices and bad decisions. Wisdom is necessary for heads of households, heads of ministries, and heads of nations. Pray for God to wisdom and holiness to all leaders.

Before looking at the author of Wisdom's prayer attributed to Solomon, look at the two historical accounts of King Solomon's prayers, which were spoken to God about ten centuries before the Book of the Wisdom of Solomon was penned.

And Solomon said, "You have shown great and merciful love to your servant David my father, because he walked before you in faithfulness, in righteousness, and in uprightness of heart toward you; and you have kept for him this great and merciful love, and have given him a son to sit on his throne this day. And now, O LORD my God, you have made your servant king in place of David my father, although I am but a little child; I do not know how to go out or come in. And your servant is in the midst of your people whom you have chosen, a great people, that cannot be numbered or counted for multitude. Give your servant therefore an understanding mind to govern your people, that I may discern between good and evil; for who is able to govern this great people of yours?" (1 Kings 3:6–9)	*And Solomon said to God, "You have shown great and merciful love to David my father, and have made me king in his stead. O LORD God, let your promise to David my father be now fulfilled, for you have made me king over a people as many as the dust of the earth. Give me now wisdom and knowledge to go out and come in before this people, for who can rule this your people, that is so great?"* (2 Chronicles 1:8–10)

Solomon demonstrates in his prayer that he preferred wisdom over and above power, wealth, material possessions, heirs, and health. He prayed to God for wisdom, in order to rule well. God granted Solomon his request; he received wisdom. Moreover, God cannot be outdone in generosity. He also gave Solomon many other things, which he had not requested. God gave Solomon power, riches, health, offspring, and material possessions along with the gift of wisdom. So great was Solomon's wisdom and prosperity that the Queen of Sheba remarked, *"The report was true which I heard in my own land of your affairs and of your wisdom, but I did not believe the reports until I came and my own eyes had seen it; and behold, the half was not told me; your wisdom and prosperity surpass the report which I heard"* (1 Kings 10:6–7). Solomon also enjoyed a forty-year reign as king in Jerusalem (1 Kings 11:42).

The Wisdom author says *Therefore be instructed by my words, and you will profit* (Wisdom 6:25). Solomon prays to God: *May God grant that I speak with judgment and have thoughts worthy of what I have received, for he is the guide even of wisdom and the corrector of the wise* (Wisdom 7:15). Here the author makes a complete distinction between wisdom, which is an attribute of God and a gift of God, and God Himself. God alone is God. And although wisdom is tied closely to God, wisdom should not be seen as somehow the same as God. Wisdom must be viewed only as an attribute or characteristic of the divine.

Characteristics of wisdom — Solomon's discourse here entails seven paragraphs, with the twenty-one characteristics of wisdom falling in the middle at Wisdom 7:22–23. Seven is the number of perfection and three is the divine number. So, seven (perfection) times three (the divine) equals twenty-one (divine perfection). Look at the attributes of wisdom described here.

... wisdom the fashioner of all things, taught me.
    For in her there is a spirit that is

1) *intelligent,*	8) *unpolluted,*	15) *humane,*
2) *holy,*	9) *distinct,*	16) *steadfast,*
3) *unique,*	10) *invulnerable,*	17) *sure,*
4) *manifold,*	11) *loving the good,*	18) *free from anxiety,*
5) *subtle,*	12) *keen,*	19) *all-powerful,*
6) *mobile,*	13) *irresistible,*	20) *overseeing all,*
7) *clear,*	14) *beneficent,*	21) *penetrating through all spirits that are intelligent and pure and most subtle.*

Here in Wisdom, the author personifies wisdom as a being separate from God. This same strategy can also be seen in Proverbs 1–9. *I, wisdom, dwell in prudence, ...The Lord created me at the beginning of his work* (Proverbs 8:12, 22). This personification of wisdom is also part and parcel of Sirach. *Wisdom will praise herself and is honored in God ... in the assembly of the Most High she will open her mouth* (Sirach 24:1–2). Although wisdom is not synonymous with God, wisdom comes from God and reflects His glory. In the Book of Sirach, wisdom is almost identical with the Law, which expresses perfectly the will of God.

Immortality — Eternal life appears in the middle part of Wisdom, as it did earlier in the book. Wisdom is a gift from God and immortality is also a gift from God. Even at this period of revelation, God had placed in the heart of people the idea of looking forward to something after the grave. Some of the psalms express a hope of life with God beyond death. *I am continually with you; you hold my right hand. You guide me with your counsel, and afterward you will receive me to glory. Whom have I in heaven but you?* (Psalm 73:23–25). The Wisdom author believes that because of wisdom, he will *have immortality and leave an everlasting remembrance to those who come after* (Wisdom 8:13), and *in kinship with wisdom there is immortality* (Wisdom 8:17).

Every child created by God ponders some very basic questions in life. Who am I? Where did I come from? Why am I here? Where am I going? How will I get there? Those questions are frequently asked of strangers who are traveling. The answers to those questions frame human lives and give meaning to life. If a person believes that nothing exists after death, that person will behave differently than if he believes that something awaits him beyond the grave. Wisdom will help the person answer those questions well and live truthfully and righteously.

Wisdom in Salvation History — Wisdom is God's providence. God has used wisdom to guide salvation history according to the divine plan. The author of Wisdom demonstrates clear knowledge of the history of the Chosen People and shows how God protected His people through the personification of wisdom. He uses a literary genre called "midrash" in which he gives a free or rather loose commentary on the scriptures. The faithful Jew would recognize the figures and events described in Wisdom 10, although the author paints in very broad strokes and refrains from offering the names of the biblical heroes.

Wisdom protected the first-formed father of the world, *when he alone had been created;* (Wisdom 10:1)	Adam
He perished because in rage he slew his brother. (Wisdom 10:3)	Cain
When the earth was flooded because of him, *wisdom again saved it, steering the righteous man* (Wisdom 10:4)	Noah
Wisdom ... recognized the righteous man ... and kept him strong *in the face of his compassion for his child.* (Wisdom 10:5)	Abraham
He escaped the fire that descended on the Five Cities. (Wisdom 10:6)	Lot
When a righteous man fled from his brother's wrath, she guided *him ... and gave him knowledge of angels;* (Wisdom 10:10)	Jacob
When a righteous man was sold, wisdom did not desert him, (Wisdom 10:13)	Joseph

She entered the soul of a servant of the Lord,
    and withstood dread kings with wonders and signs.
                                                    (Wisdom 10:16)
	Moses

The beauty of wisdom can be clearly seen in the history of the Chosen People. There is no need to run after pagan mythology or new philosophies. God has been present in the history of His people and He continues to give wisdom and immortality to those who seek Him with a pure heart.

Light, it is said in the Psalms, is the mantle with which God covers himself (Psalm 104:2). In the Book of Wisdom, the symbolism of light is used to describe the very essence of God: wisdom, an outpouring of his glory, is "a reflection of eternal light" superior to any created light (Wisdom 7:27, 29ff).

In the New Testament, it is Christ who constitutes the full manifestation of God's light. His Resurrection defeated the power of the darkness of evil forever. With the Risen Christ, truth and love triumph over deceit and sin. In him, God's light henceforth illumines definitively human life and the course of history: *"I am the light of the world,"* he says in the Gospel, *"he who follows me will not walk in darkness, but will have the light of life"* (John 8:12).

Pope Benedict XVI, *Angelus Address*, August 6, 2006.

1. What would help to save the world? Wisdom 6:24–25

2. Identify a virtue found in Wisdom 7:1–6.

3. How did Solomon attain wisdom? Wisdom 7:7; 8:21; CCC 216

4. What happens in the following passages?

Wisdom 7:8–9	
Wisdom 7:10	
Wisdom 7:11–14	

5. Where should scientific questions lead us? Wisdom 7:16–20, CCC 283

6. List twenty-one characteristics of wisdom. Wisdom 7:22–23
* Circle the ones you possess. Highlight the ones you desire.

7. What can you learn about God from Wisdom 7:24–28?

8. Describe some characteristics of truth, beauty, and goodness.

Wisdom 7:29–8:8	
CCC 2500	

9. What special gift does wisdom bring? Wisdom 8:13, 17

10. How does it feel to live with wisdom? Wisdom 8:16

11. Why did Solomon pray as he did? Wisdom 9:1–4, 11–12

12. What can you learn from the following verses?

Wisdom 9:6	
1 Corinthians 3:18–21	

13. How long has wisdom been around?

Wisdom 9: 9	
Psalm 104:24	
CCC 295	

14. How can you deal with the uncertainties and ambiguities of life?

Wisdom 9:16–17	
Sirach 1:3–7	
John 3:12–13, 21	

15. If you could see God today, what major question would you ask Him?

16. Who was the unbelieving soul?

Genesis 19:26	
Wisdom 10:7	
Luke 17:32–33	

17. What did wisdom do for the righteous man Jacob? Wisdom 10:10–12

18. What did wisdom do for the righteous man Joseph? Wisdom 10:13–14

19. Find an appropriate response to God's wisdom and protection.

Exodus 15:1–21	
Wisdom 10:20	

20. Who can even achieve wisdom and eloquence? Wisdom 10:21

Psalm 8:1-5	
Matthew 11:25–27	

CHAPTER 17

God's Providence and Mercy
Wisdom 11–19

For in everything, O LORD, you have exalted
and glorified your people;
and you have not neglected to help them
at all times and in all places.
Wisdom 19:22

Wisdom shows God's providence and mercy in history — God's mercy and justice are evident in the history of the Chosen People. Looking back at what God has done in the past can help a person gain a true perspective on the present and plan for the future. For those Jews living in Egypt, experiencing new philosophies and pagan religions, the Wisdom author presents a recollection of the story of Israel, a history lesson. In a series of contrasts, he shows how God used the very same elements either to punish His enemies, or to provide for His friends. God is just and merciful, and everything He does is done out of love. By the patience God showed to Pharaoh and the Egyptians prior to the Exodus, God teaches the Jews to imitate Him in tempering justice with mercy, and to hope for mercy themselves.

But you, our God, are kind and true,
patient and ruling all things in mercy.
For even if we sin we are yours, knowing your power;
but we will not sin, because we know that we are considered yours.
For to know you is complete righteousness,
and to know your power is the root of immortality.
Wisdom 15:1–3

Egypt in the first century BC was a hotbed of idolatry, with the orgiastic rites of Dionysius and many pagan cults with practices offered to various Greek gods and goddesses. Idolatry is always a serious offense against God, whether one chooses to worship nature or a false idol created by human hands. Remaining faithful to the covenant of the One True God in the midst of a pagan culture requires courage and fidelity. The author of Wisdom endeavors to support those Jews who are faithful to God in the diaspora and to call back to the truth those who have wandered into the idolatrous practices around them.

Contrasts — *For through the very things by which their enemies were punished, they themselves received benefit in their need* (Wisdom 11:5). Wisdom preserved the people of Israel when they were in bondage in Egypt many centuries before. The story of the slavery of the Jews to Pharaoh in Egypt would have been told from generation to generation. Recalling their hardships set the stage for the dramatic and magnificent work of God in bringing the Chosen People to the Promised Land.

Water — Water is necessary for life. God used water to sustain and satisfy the thirst of His people in the desert. But, God also used that very same element—water—to punish the Egyptians. Once water had been the means the Egyptians used to torment the Hebrews, when Pharaoh ordered the midwives to drown the baby boys. In the very first plague, God commanded Moses and Aaron to turn the water of the Nile River into blood. All the fish died and the water became polluted, unfit for drinking (Exodus 7:14–24). So the Egyptians were forced to dig wells to sustain life, since they could not drink from the river. In contrast, when the Israelites were thirsty in the desert God told Moses to command a rock to yield, from which fresh water gushed forth in abundance. So, water, which sustained the Israelites, was also used to punish the Egyptians (Wisdom 11:4–6).

> *For you tested them as a father does in warning,*
> *but you examined the ungodly*
> *as a stern king does in condemnation.*
> Wisdom 11:10

Wildlife — Animals provide food and nourishment for man, but wildlife can also be pests, destroying crops and eating the very food that man needs to harvest to survive. The Egyptians worshipped a series of living things, including crocodiles, serpents, lizards and frogs. This type of idolatry is abhorrent to God. It is not surprising that God used the very things that the Egyptians worshipped to punish them in the plagues of the frogs, gnats, flies, and locusts (Exodus 7–10).

Wisdom offers a profound commentary on the Exodus plague. "*You sent upon them a multitude of irrational creatures to punish them, that they might learn that one is punished by the very things by which he sins* (Wisdom 11:15–16). Sin is often its own punishment. The alcoholic suffers from alcohol. The glutton suffers health problems as the result of too much rich food. The adulterer may suffer disease and the loss of beloved family members. The idolater suffers by the very thing he worships and adores. Yet, God uses the wildlife to bless and sustain Israel when he sends quail in the desert to alleviate their hunger (Exodus 16:13).

Weather and the elements — rain, hail, and fire — God destroyed the crops of the Egyptians with thunderbolts of lightning (fire), downpours of rain, and severe hail storms (Exodus 9:22–27). In contrast, God rained down manna from heaven, *the bread of the angels* (Psalm 78:25) to feed the hungry Jewish people in the desert. The manna assumed many various flavors, and fire did not melt it when it was being cooked. So, God sent the fire from heaven that destroyed the food of the Egyptians, but God provided food from heaven for His people that fire would not destroy (Wisdom 16:18–20).

Darkness and light — The ninth plague of the Egyptians was total darkness over the entire land (Exodus 10:21–28), which was so severe that people could not move from place to place for three days. The Egyptians were imprisoned by darkness, fear, and panic. In contrast, God led Israel through the desert with a pillar of fire to light their way. Moses would bring the light of the Law for the Chosen People to follow. And ultimately, from this people would come Jesus the Messiah, who would announce, *"I am the light of the world; he who follows me will not walk in darkness, but will have the light of life"* (John 8:12). Neither the people living at the time of the Exodus, nor the people living in the time of the Wisdom writer could even imagine that God would send such a Redeemer.

Later still, the beloved disciple John would explain that *God is light and in him is no darkness at all. If we say we have fellowship with him while we walk in darkness, we lie and do not live according to the truth; but if we walk in the light, as he is in the light, we have fellowship with one another, and the blood of Jesus his Son cleanses us from all sin* (1 John 1:6–7). God has sent the light of His revelation into the world in gradual ways. People are expected to follow the best light that God has given them in whatever time and place they happen to live. Righteous people seek the light of truth and wisdom. The unrighteous reject the light of truth because they prefer to remain in the darkness of sin (John 3:19–21).

Death of the children and men — Pharaoh ordered the midwives to kill the Hebrew baby boys by drowning them in the river (Exodus 1:15–22; Wisdom 18:5). God rescued baby Moses from the river. The midwives feared God rather than obey Pharaoh. In contrast, the firstborn son of Pharaoh, along with the firstborn sons of all of his subjects, suffered the horrors of death on the night of Passover. Only the firstborn sons of the Israelites, who had the blood of the lamb on the lintels of their doorposts, were spared. There was wailing and mourning throughout Egypt (Exodus 12:29–30; Wisdom 18:10–13). Moreover, those who had used the Nile River in an attempt to drown Israel's children were themselves drowned in the Red Sea along with their chariots as they pursued Moses and the people through the Red Sea (Exodus 14:23–31; Wisdom 10:18–20).

The catastrophic events of the first Passover are almost too horrific to imagine. Mothers and fathers wailed in mourning as they buried their firstborn sons—the hope of their future. And scarcely had the burials been completed, when the fathers of many of those same families would be called out to man the chariots in pursuit of Israel. How many mothers who had buried sons would now bury a husband or father or brother? So much grief and suffering were endured by a people whose leader had hardened his heart against God and refused to follow the light that was offered to him. One man's refusal to repent causes suffering to countless others.

Conscience — *For wickedness is a cowardly thing, condemned by its own testimony; distressed by* **conscience**, *it has always exaggerated the difficulties. For fear is nothing but surrender of the helps that come from reason* (Wisdom 17:11–12). The word "conscience" appears for the first time in the Bible here in Wisdom. Conscience is the still, small voice in a human being, within whose heart the inner law of God is inscribed. Conscience bears witness to the truth and discriminates between those acts that are good and those that are evil. Even before the Ten Commandments were given, Joseph knew in his heart that it was wrong for him to betray his master and give in to Potiphar's wife (Genesis 39). In primitive cultures which have never seen a Bible, nor heard about God, there are prohibitions against murder, lying, and stealing. So, God has placed a conscience in each human heart.

Pharaoh hardened his heart and dulled his conscience. Even though the Ten Commandments had not yet been given to Moses, a still, small voice must have cried out for the lives of the innocent Hebrew baby boys about to be thrown into the sea. God writes His law on the human heart. But, free will allows the heart to be hardened and the conscience to be dulled and compromised. The expectation for the God-seeking person is to form one's conscience according to God's law and His perfect will. "Following one's conscience" has come to mean "following your whims or feelings," or "doing whatever seems good to you" (Romans 2:14–16).

In Psalm 19:12–13, we find the ever-worth-pondering passage, *But who can discern his errors? Clear me from my unknown faults.* That is not Old Testament objectivism, but profoundest human wisdom. No longer seeing one's guilt, the falling silent of conscience in so many areas is an even more dangerous sickness of the soul than the guilt that one still recognizes as such. He who no longer notices that killing is a sin has fallen farther than the one who still recognizes the shamefulness of his actions, because the former is further removed from the truth and conversion.

Not without reason does the self-righteous man in the encounter with Jesus appear as the one who is really lost. If the tax collector with all his undisputed sins stands more justified before God than the Pharisee with all his undeniably good works (Luke 18:9–14), this is not because the sins of the tax collector were not sins or because the good deeds of the Pharisee were not good deeds. Nor does it mean that the good that man does is not good before God, or the evil, not evil …

The reason for this paradoxical judgment of God is shown precisely from our question. The Pharisee no longer knows that he too has guilt. He has a completely clear conscience. But the silence of conscience makes him impenetrable to God and men, while the cry of conscience that plagues the tax collector makes him capable of truth and love. Jesus can move sinners. Not hiding behind the screen of their erroneous consciences, they have not become unreachable for the change that God expects of them—of us. He is ineffective with the "righteous" because they are not aware of any need for forgiveness and conversion. Their consciences no longer accuse them, but justify them.

Pope Benedict XVI, *On Conscience*
(San Francisco: Ignatius Press, 2007), pp. 18–19

Evil is a cowardly thing. The author of Wisdom endeavors to call the people of God back to faithfulness, in the midst of a pagan society. Salvation history provides many examples of God's faithfulness to His people. His mercy and love are everlasting. God's justice on the evildoers is also sobering. God is not mocked. Those who harden their hearts and refuse to form their consciences and follow God's laws receive punishment. The authors of the wisdom literature expected punishments to be meted out in this lifetime. But, God had placed a hint in their minds that perhaps something would happen beyond the grave. Immortality was a new concept for Israel. Perhaps rewards and punishments would come after this life. The people in the diaspora were trying to keep faith in a pagan environment. People today must also try to keep faith in an environment hostile to God.

1. Find some examples of divine providence contrasted with divine punishment.

Wisdom 11:1–5	
Wisdom 11:6–14	
Exodus 16:1–13	
Wisdom 11:15–26	

2. Give two examples of something that was used at one time as a blessing in your life, and at another time the same thing was used as punishment.

3. Why would God use the same means to punish some and reward others?

Wisdom 11:16	
Wisdom 11:21	
Wisdom 11:23	
Wisdom 11:26	
Psalm 103:17–19	

4. Identify some characteristics of God.

Wisdom 11:10	
Wisdom 11:21	
CCC 269	
Wisdom 11:23	
Wisdom 12:18	
Wisdom 12:22	

5. Which characteristic of God above do you find most comforting?

6. How did God create the world?

Genesis 1:31	
Wisdom 11:20	
CCC 299	

7. From Wisdom 13:1–9, what conclusion should people draw about God?

8. Name the sin found below.

Exodus 20:3–6	
Wisdom 13:10–19	

9. List some types of idolatry common today.

10. To whom or what could the following verses refer?

Wisdom 14:3–4	
Wisdom 14:7	

11. What does Wisdom tell you about God?

Wisdom 15:1–2	
Psalm 86:5	
Psalm 86:15–17	
Psalm 145:8–13	

12. What truth can you glean from these passages?

Wisdom 15:3	
John 17:3	

13. Identify the events alluded to in these passages.

Wisdom 15:18–16:1; 19:10	
Exodus 8:1–2, 13, 20	
Wisdom 16:2–3	

14. Have you ever experienced God providing something miraculously?

15. What does the manna prefigure?

Psalm 78:23–25	
Psalm 105:40	
Wisdom 16:20–22	
John 6:31–35	
John 6:51–58	
CCC 1374	

* How do you prepare yourself to receive the Eucharist? How do you give thanks?

16. Identify the events in the following passages.

Wisdom 17:1–10	
Wisdom 18:1–4	

17. Define "conscience." Wisdom 17:11, CCC 1777–1778

18. How can you form your conscience?

Psalm 119:97–105	
CCC 1779	
CCC 1783–1784	
CCC 1785	
CCC 1789	

19. What can cause errors of judgment? CCC 1791–1792

20. Use the Commandments to write an Examination of Conscience. Exodus 20

I	
II	
III	
IV	
V	
VI	
VII	
VIII	
IX	
X	

CHAPTER 18

Wisdom in the Law
Sirach 1–10

To fear the Lord is wisdom's full measure;
she satisfies men with her fruits;
she fills their whole house with desirable goods,
and their storehouses with her produce.
The fear of the Lord is the crown of wisdom,
making peace and perfect health to flourish...
If you desire wisdom, keep the commandments.
Sirach 1:16–18, 26

In about 195 BC, *Jeshua ben Eleazar ben Sira,* "Jesus son of Eleazar son of Sira," a faithful Jew and renown teacher, commonly called "Ben Sira" wrote a compendium of his class lecture notes and reflections, which would later become one of the Wisdom books of the Bible. Ben Sira was the master of an academy in Jerusalem. He taught young scribes how to attain wisdom by fearing the Lord and obeying the Torah. He did not labor for himself alone, but rather he wrote this book *for all who seek instruction* (Sirach 33:17).

The Book of Sirach, originally written in Hebrew and translated into Greek by the author's grandson, was also translated into Aramaic and Syriac. The Hebrew text was lost over the centuries, although large portions of the Hebrew manuscript were recovered in Cairo, Egypt and Masada and Qumran, Israel. Some fragments have even been discovered as recently as 2008 in a library in Cambridge, England.

About sixty years later (around 132 BC), an unnamed grandson of Ben Sira translated his grandfather's book into Greek for the diaspora Jews, probably living in Alexandria, Egypt, at that time. The title "Sirach" is an abbreviation of the longer title, which was found in the Greek manuscripts. The Latin Vulgate translation of the Bible uses the title *Ecclesiasticus,* which means literally the "Church book." This title still appears in some translations, including the Jerusalem Bible. So, if Sirach does not appear in a Bible table of contents, look for the title Ecclesiasticus, distinct from Ecclesiastes, another Wisdom book previously studied.

A novelty of the book, reflecting the Hellenistic influence of the time, is that the author does not shy away from claiming his authorship. However, there is a problem with his precise name. Although the opening chapters with a possible title have not been preserved in Hebrew, there is a very informative colophon at the very end of the book (after Sirach 51, which actually appears to be an addition to Sirach 50 that already had a colophon of its own: Sirach 50:27–29). In the Hebrew versions this colophon after Sirach 51:30 is given as: "*Til here go the words of <u>Simon</u>, son of Joshua, who* *is called Ben Sira. Wisdom of <u>Simon</u>, son of Joshua, son of Eleazar, son of Sira.*" The difference in the Hebrew and Greek translations can be illustrated by looking at the original colophon at the end of Sirach 50.

Hebrew	*Discipline of knowledge and balanced direction,* *by Simon, son of Joshua, son of Eleazar, son of Sira;* *which his heart brought forth as an explanation* *and which he has spread with understanding (Sirach 50:27).*
Greek	*Instruction in understanding and knowledge* *I have written in this book,* *Jesus the son of Sirach Eleazar, the Jerusalemite,* *who out of his heart poured forth wisdom (Sirach 50:27).*

This conflicting evidence goes beyond what the grandson already remarked in his forward, namely that *"what was originally expressed in Hebrew does not have exactly the same sense when translated into another language."* There seems to be another force at work here. Not long after the book was completed, the high priestly dynasty of Simon lost its power to the Hasmoneans, and it seems that some reviser tried to bring the book up-to-date by removing the name of the high priest Simon from Sirach 50:24 onward. This revision found its way into the Greek translation, which omits the name Simon in Sirach 50:24 and instead reads "with us." In the stride of this actualization the first colophon may also have been revised, but here "Simon" referred not to the high priest but to the author.

The name of the author has usually been interpreted from the Greek text and it has often been assumed "Simon" is an addition to the Hebrew version and that the author's name is "Jesus," his father's name is Sirach, and his grandfather's name is Eleazar. The reason the Greek versions traditionally have held preference has to do with the formation of the canon in Christianity and in Judaism. For the rest of this Bible study, the Greek text that was used in translating the RSVCE is used.

In the prologue, the grandson reveals that his grandfather endeavored to study the Law, the prophets, and the writings of our ancestors. This insight suggests that the traditional threefold division of the Hebrew Scriptures into *TANAK*—the Law, the prophets, and the writings—was known as early as the late second century BC.

TANAK, or *TANAKH* is the term used among Jews for the Hebrew Bible.
1) "<u>T</u>or<u>a</u>h" – The Law is found in the Torah or Pentateuch, which includes the first five books of the Bible.
2) "<u>N</u>ebi'im" – The Prophets are those holy men who spoke and wrote God's word, and frequently foretold future events in Israel's history.
3) "<u>K</u>et<u>h</u>ubim" – The Writings, or Hagiographa include the other sacred writings, including the psalms and wisdom literature.

At the time this book was written (the second century BC), the list of sacred books within Judaism was net yet definite. The list of books of the first two sections, the Law and the Prophets, was already fixed, but the list of books in the third section, written in the format of poetic verse, was not yet set. At roughly the same time, the need was felt within Judaism for a Greek version of the sacred books, because too many Jews in the diaspora could no longer understand biblical Hebrew. Eleazer, the Jewish high priest, chose six scholars from each of the twelve tribes of Israel to translate the Hebrew Scriptures into Greek. Since the total number of scholars was seventy-two, their joint translation was called the "Septuagint," abbreviated LXX.

With regard to the third section of the canon, the Septuagint translation had a slightly different list of books. There is no evidence that in the pre-Christian era the two lists posed a problem for Judaism, and this situation continued as long as Christians were a minority within Palestinian Aramaic-speaking Jewry. When Christianity outgrew the Palestinian context and adopted Greek as its main language, it naturally read the Scriptures according to the Septuagint canon.

The destruction of the Temple in AD 70 and the fact that Jews were forbidden entrance into Jerusalem, together with the rapid spread of Christianity with its own sacred books, made it necessary for Judaism to establish its own canon of sacred books. The formation of the Jewish canon occurred at the end of the first century AD (when the New Testament had already been written). In spite of its huge popularity among Jewish readers (Sirach is often quoted in the Talmud and rabbinic writings), the Wisdom of Ben Sira did not make it into that canon.

Reasons for the exclusion of Sirach from the Jewish canon are not documented. One reason may be that it was obviously written after the assumed end of the prophetic inspiration period. In the first century AD, the Pharisees and the Jewish historian Flavius Josephus held that prophetic inspiration died out after Ezra and Nehemiah. Another reason may be that even in its Hebrew version, the book underwent several revisions reflecting changes that occurred in the second and first century BC Judaism, but which were not continued in Judaism after the first century AD.

The Greek translation of the Hebrew Scriptures, the Septuagint, contained several sacred books that were venerated by the Greek-speaking Jews in the diaspora, but were missing from the canon in Jerusalem. The Christian people embraced the Septuagint as their own and accepted these books as divinely inspired into the canon of Sacred Scripture. These books, called deutero-canonical, include: Wisdom, Sirach, Judith, Esther, Tobit, Baruch, 1 and 2 Maccabees, and additional chapters of Daniel. Catholics and Orthodox Christians accept the above books.

Sirach resembles Proverbs in style and content. The poetic device of the balanced, pithy proverb, a short saying of two lines in either synonymous or opposite parallels, and the distinctive poetic writing style are evident in both books. The personification of Wisdom which was seen in Proverbs 8:22–9:12 and Wisdom 7:22–30, also appears in Sirach 24:1–34.

Ben Sira distinguishes himself from the authors of Proverbs and Qoheleth by emphasizing the importance of the Torah. He recalls the prophets and the ancient heroes of Israel in recounting their role in the history of salvation. Ben Sira also brings his teaching to a higher theological plane by breaking into hymns and prayers to God, much as the Psalmist would do (Sirach 23:1–6; 36:1–17; 51:1–12). In this way, he is more than a wisdom teacher to his scribes. Ben Sira is a spiritual father showing his disciples how to pray to God.

Sirach does not lend itself well to clear divisions or an outline. Many chapters break in the middle of a developing thought or theme. One exception is the very clear outline praising the ancient heroes of Israel (Sirach 44–50). Ben Sira addresses several topics, which he revisits and develops more fully throughout the book. Therefore, the division of several chapters at a time is given simply to make it possible to work through this long book over several weeks. The divisions may come at an inopportune time, and revisiting previous chapters will be necessary to thoroughly study important topics. Sirach seems to reach spiritual heights in the beginning, middle, and end. It opens with a plea to fear the Lord, pray for wisdom, and obey the law of God, and ends with a reflection on the magnificence of God's creation, a retelling of the faith of Israel's leaders, and the example of the high priest. In the middle a poem describes wisdom's dwelling place in Jerusalem (Sirach 24:1–34), and another shows the role of the scribe in praising God (Sirach 39:1–15).

AMONG SOME MAJOR THEMES ADDRESSED IN SIRACH ARE:		
Creation	Sirach	16:24–17:24; 18:1–14; 33:7–15; 39:12–35; 42:15–43:33.
Family	Sirach	3:1–16; 7:23–25; 16:1–4; 30:1–13; 41:5–10; 42:9–14.
Friends	Sirach	6:5–17; 9:10–16; 19:13–17; 22:19–26; 27:16–21.
Honor	Sirach	4:20–6:4; 10:9–11:6; 41:14–42:8.
Manners	Sirach	31:12–32:13; 37:27–31.
Money	Sirach	3:30–4:10; 11:7–28; 13:1–14:19; 29:1–28; 31:1–11.
Sin	Sirach	7:1–17; 15:11–20; 16:1–17:31; 18:30–19:3; 21:1–10; 22:27–23:27; 26:28–28:7.
Speech	Sirach	5:9–15; 18:15–29; 19:4–17; 20:1–31; 23:7–15; 27:4–15; 28:8–26.
Women	Sirach	3:4, 3:11; 7:19–26; 9:1–9; 22:3–5; 23:22–26; 25:1, 8, 13; 23:16–26:27; 28:15; 36:25; 37:11; 40:19–23; 42:9–14.

The numbering of verses is markedly different in several places in the New American Bible (NAB) and the Revised Standard Version Catholic Edition (RSVCE). This has to do with the fact that in an early stage of the tradition, several chapters switched places in the Greek translation. When translating, sometimes the Greek translators follow the original Hebrew order of chapters and verses. The verses referenced in this book will refer specifically to the RSVCE.

The most important theme addressed by Ben Sira is the relationship between wisdom and God's law. The word wisdom appears more than sixty times in Sirach. Ben Sira sought wisdom from his youth (Sirach 51:13–14). He strove to live according to God's law and to attain wisdom, so that he could give glory to God (Sirach 51:17). A major objective for Ben Sira was to transmit the religious culture to the young. He wanted his scribes to seek wisdom and achieve virtue, to be obedient to the Law, and in so doing to give glory to God. The term "my son" (Sirach 2:1) is the loving term a spiritual father addresses to his disciple or student. The seeker of wisdom is therefore "the son."

All wisdom is the fear of the Lord, and in all wisdom there is the fulfillment of the law (Sirach 19:20). Those who fear the Lord and obey His law can find true wisdom. Wisdom is a gift of God that was created by God in the beginning. *The Lord himself created wisdom in the holy spirit* (Sirach 1:9). Ben Sira identifies the source of all wisdom and the existing attitude necessary to obtain wisdom.

The virtue of humility underscores the life of the wisdom seeker. The "fear of the Lord" is mentioned forty-one times in the Book of Sirach. Fear of the Lord is an attitude of profound reverence, awe, and respect due to Almighty God, the Creator of the world. It acknowledges the power, majesty, and sovereignty of God.

> This attitude of faith leads men and women to recognize the power of God who works in history and thus to open themselves to feeling awe for the name of the Lord. In biblical language, in fact, this "fear" is not fright, it does not denote fear, for fear of God is something quite different. It is recognition of the mystery of divine transcendence. Thus, it is at the root of faith and is interwoven with love. Sacred Scripture says in Deuteronomy: *What does the Lord, your God, ask of you but to fear the Lord, your God, and … to love … the Lord, your God, with all your heart and all your soul* (Deuteronomy 10:12). As Saint Hilary of Poitiers, a fourth-century bishop, said: "All our fear is in love."
>
> Pope Benedict XVI, *General Audience* (May 11, 2005)

Some of the ways in which Ben Sira speaks of the fear of the Lord are:

To fear the Lord is the beginning of wisdom	Sirach 1:14
To fear the Lord is wisdom's full measure	Sirach 1:16
The fear of the Lord is the crown of wisdom	Sirach 1:18

Those who fear the Lord will not disobey his words Sirach 2:15
Those who fear the Lord will seek his approval Sirach 2:16
With all your soul fear the Lord Sirach 7:29
He that fears the Lord will repent in his heart Sirach 21:6b
Nothing is better than fear of the Lord Sirach 23:27
The fear of the Lord is like a garden of blessing Sirach 40:27

The man who fears the Lord and seeks after wisdom will obey the commandments and uphold the law of God. *Blessed is the man who meditates on wisdom …The man who fears the Lord will do this, and he who holds to the law will obtain wisdom* (Sirach 14:20, 15:1). In order to become wise, the seeker of wisdom must listen and obey. Ben Sira encourages the seeker of wisdom to search for good counsel, to find wise mentors, and to listen to them. *The source of wisdom is God's word in the highest heaven, and her ways are the eternal commandments* (Sirach 1:5). How can one obey God and please God? Ben Sira admonishes his disciples who love learning to make even greater progress by living according to the Law. So study God's word, obey His commandments and become wise.

1. From where does wisdom come?

Sirach 1:1	
Sirach 1:5	
Sirach 1:9	

2. What lesson can you find in Sirach 1:22–25?

3. Why should you avoid pride? Sirach 1:30; Proverbs 16:18

4. Describe the fear of the Lord.

Sirach 1:14	
Sirach 2:7–17	
Sirach 6:16–17	
Sirach 7:29–31	
Sirach 10:20	

5. What can you learn from the following passages?

Sirach 2:1–5	
James 1:2–3	

6. What must the one who desires wisdom do?

Sirach 1:26	
Sirach 2:10–16	
Sirach 6:37	
Sirach 15:1, 15	

7. Identify an activity necessary to growing in wisdom. Sirach 6:32–37

* Describe a practical way can you apply the direction given above.

8. List some specific instructions given in Sirach 3.

9. Identify a corporal work of mercy from Sirach 4.

10. What sacrament fulfills Sirach 4:25–26? CCC 1422, 1423, 1424

* When is the next time you could celebrate the Sacrament of Reconciliation?

11. Put Sirach 5:1 into your own words.

12. Describe the activity desired in Sirach 5:7–8. CCC 821

13. List some sins of the tongue from Sirach 5:9–15.

* What problems with the tongue are most difficult for you to manage?

14. Explain Sirach 6:5 in your own words.

15. Write three warnings from Sirach 7 that could apply to you personally.

16. Find three cautions in Sirach 8 that could apply to you.

17. From Sirach 9, list three verses that strike you and explain why.

18. What sin is identified in Sirach 10:12–13?

* What practical thing can you do to counteract that deadly sin?

19. Who is worthy of honor? Sirach 10:19–20

20. With what virtue can you glorify yourself? Sirach 10:27–28

CHAPTER 19

Family and Friends
Sirach 11–22

A faithful friend is a sturdy shelter:
he that has found one has found a treasure.
There is nothing so precious as a faithful friend,
and no scales can measure his excellence.
A faithful friend is an elixir of life;
and those who fear the Lord will find him.
Whoever fears the Lord directs his friendship aright,
for as he is, so is his neighbor also.
Sirach 6:14–17

The Book of Sirach could be called a handbook of practical wisdom for living a life pleasing to God. Ben Sira demonstrates a concern for interpersonal relationships among men and women, in marriage and family life, between husband and wife, parents and children, and among friends. Indeed no book of the Bible has as much to say about friendship as the Book of Sirach. Friends and family concerns transcend cultures and generations. The wisdom Ben Sira prescribed over 2000 years ago still provides application for the lives of God-fearing people today.

Marriage and family life are the bedrock of society. As marriage and family life go, so the society goes. When marriages and children are protected, the society is strong. When marriage and family life are threatened, the society suffers greatly. Contemporary society demonstrates that government and social institutions cannot supply the love and security that an intact marriage and strong family can provide. Orphanages and foster-care situations may be necessary to provide for the abandoned, but they are not God's primary plan. Ben Sira also shows concern for the widow and orphan. *Be like a father to orphans and instead of a husband to their mother; you will then be like a son of the Most High, and he will love you more than does your mother* (Sirach 4:10). Marriage, the primary societal unit, was the first institution created by God. Those are blessed who can go beyond the needs of their own families to care for the less fortunate. But, the care of one's own marriage and family takes primary concern before corporal works of mercy.

My soul takes pleasure in three things, and they are beautiful in the sight of the Lord and of men: agreement between brothers, friendship between neighbors, and a wife and husband who live in harmony (Sirach 25:1). Ben Sira seems to state the obvious. Loving family relationships between husband and wife and between siblings are pleasing to God and beautiful in the sight of everyone. People enjoy going to weddings and rejoice with the bride and groom. How much more wonderful it is to celebrate the twenty-fifth or fiftieth anniversary of a faithful married couple who have weathered the trials and storms of life over the years!

Perhaps the most beautiful passage concerning marriage can be found in Sirach 26: *Happy is the husband of a good wife; the number of his days will be doubled. A loyal wife rejoices her husband, and he will complete his years in peace. A good wife is a great blessing; she will be granted among the blessings of the man who fears the Lord. Whether rich or poor, his heart is glad, and at all times his face is cheerful* (Sirach 26:1–4). Ben Sira encourages the husband to enjoy the wife of his youth, and he admonishes him to avoid straying from the marital bed. *Wine and women lead intelligent men astray, and the man who consorts with harlots is very reckless* (Sirach 19:2). Adultery destroys trust and hurts adults and children. Sirach gives strong warnings to both men and women to avoid occasions of sexual sin.

Children have duties toward their parents. In the Mosaic law, God commanded children to honor their parents. *"Honor your father and your mother, that your days may be long in the land which the Lord your God gives you"* (Exodus 20:12). Ben Sira provides some additional commentary on this verse throughout his book. He offers practical wisdom for parents in training and disciplining their children. He also states clearly the responsibilities of children toward their parents, even adult children showing honor to aging parents and caring for them in their twilight years.

Whoever honors his father atones for sins, and preserves himself from them. When he prays, he is heard; and whoever glorifies his mother is like one who lays up treasure. Whoever honors his father will be gladdened by his own children, and when he prays he will be heard (Sirach 3:3–5). So, what goes around comes around. And that person can expect God to hear his prayer. And the person who shows honor to parents can expect his children to show honor and respect as well. Every parent experiences disobedient or disrespectful children, but the parent is encouraged to be strict and firm with discipline.

Parents must discipline children. Adults also strive for self-discipline. *Do you have children? Discipline them and make them obedient from their youth* (Sirach 7:23). Failure to discipline children brings shame and disgrace to parents. *It is a disgrace to be the father of an undisciplined son ... A sensible daughter obtains her husband, but one who acts shamefully brings grief to her father* (Sirach 22:3–4). The preference for sons emerges in Sirach. In agrarian societies, a son could help to work the land or tend the flocks. However, a daughter could not contribute to the family enterprise and could bring shame on her family. Recall the rape of Dinah, and the subsequent revenge of her brothers in Genesis 34. While it may sound harsh, even in contemporary society, such as China with its one-child policy, sons are preferred to carry on the family name, and daughters are often either aborted or placed for adoption.

Reading Sirach may be challenging to one's politically correct sensibilities and contemporary standards. *He who loves his son will whip him often in order that he may rejoice at the way he turns out. He who disciplines his son will profit by him, and will boast of him among acquaintances* (Sirach 30:1–2). Ben Sira is not advocating child abuse, which is quite different from corporal punishment. Rather, Ben Sira is consistent here with the author of Proverbs: *He who spares the rod hates his son, but he who loves him is diligent to discipline him* (Proverbs 13:24). Contemporary society sadly has an excessive amount of child abuse and neglect, and also an excessive number of undisciplined, unruly children. While parents may prayerfully consider which means of discipline are most effective for a given child, the parents have the responsibility to train the child and help him to grow up to be a well-disciplined adult. If the parents refuse to discipline, the teachers must try. If the teachers fail, then employers or police are left with the result and must deal with an undisciplined person.

Appropriate discipline is a manifestation of love. God disciplines His children in love. *My son, do not regard lightly the discipline of the Lord, nor lose courage when you are punished by him. For the Lord disciplines him whom he loves, and chastises every son whom he receives. It is for discipline that you have to endure. God is treating you as sons; for what son is there whom his father does not discipline? If you are left without discipline, in which all have participated, then you are illegitimate children and not sons* (Hebrews 12:5–8).

Self-discipline is the ultimate objective. In a civilized society, all members must learn to control their passions and appetites in order to live peaceably with others. Adults strive to acquire self-discipline, even as children must first receive discipline from parents. *O that whips were set over my thoughts, and the discipline of wisdom over my mind! That they may not spare me in my errors, and that it may not pass by my sins; in order that my mistakes may not be multiplied, and my sins may not abound* (Sirach 23:2–3).

God intends children to be a blessing to their parents, and children long to be blessed by their parents in return. *Honor your father by word and deed, that a blessing from him may come upon you. For a father's blessing strengthens the houses of the children* (Sirach 3:8–9). Ben Sira also instructs adult children to honor and care for their parents in their later years. The loving care of the elderly by their children brings blessings from God. *O son, help your father in his old age, and do not grieve him as long as he lives; even if he is lacking in understanding, show forbearance; and do not despise him all the days of his life. For kindness to a father will not be forgotten, and against your sins it will be credited to you* (Sirach 3:12–14).

God's Word provides much practical instruction for husbands and wives, parents and children. The thought of approaching marriage and family life according to scriptural imperatives may be challenging, but the results are beautiful to behold. A marriage and family life based on God's order and plan brings blessings for parents and children, grandparents, and friends. Indeed the whole society is blessed when marriage and family life correspond to God's purpose and plan.

Behold how good and pleasant it is when brothers dwell in unity!
It is like the precious oil upon the head, running down upon the beard,
upon the beard of Aaron, running down the collar of his robes!
Psalm 133:1–2

There is nothing so precious as a faithful friend, and no scales can measure his excellence (Sirach 6:15). A friend is someone who has a close personal relationship of mutual affection and trust with another. Most people long to have at least one good, intimate friend. No one in the Bible has more to say about friends and friendship than Ben Sira.

How can you acquire a friend? *A pleasant voice multiplies friends and softens enemies, and a gracious tongue multiplies courtesies* (Sirach 6:5). Positive, charitable speech proves to be an asset in making friends. Negative, mocking, critical speech will not help in making friends and influencing people. *Whoever fears the Lord directs his friendship aright* (Sirach 6:17). A true friend behaves righteously and wants the best for his friend. True friends act uprightly and don't lead one another into trouble. *Do not delight in what pleases the ungodly* (Sirach 9:12). Ben Sira gives matter-of-fact advice on friendship that any parent or teacher would gladly applaud.

True friends stay faithful in good times as well as in hard times. A fair weather friend appears in times of prosperity to share the good fortune, but may disappear in times of adversity or suffering. *Gain the trust of your neighbor in his poverty, that you may rejoice with him in his prosperity; stand by him in time of affliction, that you may share with him in his inheritance* (Sirach 22:23). A friend in need is a friend indeed. *For there is a friend who is such at his own convenience, but will not stand by you in your day of trouble* (Sirach 6:8). Finally, *Every friend will say, "I too am a friend;" but some friends are friends only in name* (Sirach 37:1).

Friendship occurs on many levels. There may be a friend for a season, perhaps a schoolmate, who disappears at graduation. Another childhood friend may remain faithful throughout life. Sometimes a friend might be seen infrequently, but the relationship still runs deep. David and Jonathan provide a biblical example of loyal friendship. *Jonathan made a covenant with David because he loved him as his own soul* (1 Samuel 18:3). When Jonathan learned that Saul wanted to kill David, he said: *May the Lord be with you as he has been with my father. If I am still alive, show me the loyal love of the Lord, that I may not die; and do not cut off your loyalty from my house for ever* (1 Samuel 20:13–15). David honored his promise to Jonathan after the death of his friend.

The most profound example of friendship appears in the New Testament. Jesus said, *"Greater love has no man than this, that a man lay down his life for his friends. You are my friends if you do what I command you. No longer do I call you servants, for the servant does not know what his master is doing; but I have called you friends … This I command you, to love one another"* (John 15:13–17).

Love is the basis for good interpersonal relationships in marriage, family life, and friendships. Jesus provides the most perfect example of selfless love. He gave everything, even His very life for His friends. What a friend we have in Jesus! What an example and command Jesus gives us—to love completely and selflessly.

1. What admonition is given in Sirach 11:2?

2. What practical wisdom can be found in Sirach 11:8?

3. Identify some thoughts about money from Sirach 11:11–26.

4. Identify some facts about friends and enemies from Sirach 12.

Sirach 12:1–2	
Sirach 12:4–8	
Sirach 12:9–12	
Sirach 12:16–18	

5. What can you learn about friendship from John 15:13–17?

* Describe a special friend in your life.

6. What results from a good deed done? Sirach 12:1–2

7. List three principles concerning the use of riches from Sirach 13—14.

8. What can you learn from the following passages?

Sirach 15:1, 15	
Sirach 15:11–15, 20	
Sirach 15:16–17	

* Are there any areas in which you or your family members compromise on or disregard God's law or the laws of the Church?

9. Identify some concerns for parents.

Sirach 16:1–4	
Sirach 7:23	
Sirach 7:24	
Sirach 30:1–13	

10. Describe some duties of children.

Sirach 3:3–9	
Sirach 3:11	
Sirach 3:12–14	

*In what way could you honor your parents now?

11. Explain Sirach 16:11–14 in your own words.

12. Find a promise in Sirach 17:25–29.

13. Explain Sirach 18:13–14 in your own words.

14. What can you learn about speech from these passages?

Sirach 18:15–29	
Sirach 19:4–12	
Sirach 20:1–8	
Sirach 20:13–17	
Sirach 20:18–20	
Sirach 20:24–26	
Sirach 20:27–28	

15. What can you learn from Sirach 21:17?

* In what practical way could you improve your speech?

16. What should you do about your sins? Sirach 21:1–2

17. Describe the way of sinners. Sirach 21:10

18. Paraphrase or write and memorize Sirach 22:27.

19. What can you learn from these passages?

Sirach 15:11–12	
1 Corinthians 10:13	
James 1:13–14	

* Share some effective ways you have found of dealing with temptation.

20. Explain some facts about fools and foolishness.

Sirach 21:8–9	
Sirach 21:14	
Sirach 21:16	
Sirach 21:18–19	
Sirach 22:8–13	

* Describe a well-disciplined person or family you know.

CHAPTER 20

Women
Sirach 23–32

Happy is the husband of a good wife;
the number of his days will be doubled.
A loyal wife rejoices her husband,
and he will complete his years in peace.
A good wife is a great blessing;
she will be granted among the blessings
of the man who fears the Lord.
Whether rich or poor, his heart is glad,
and at all times his face is cheerful.
Sirach 26:1–4

Ben Sira has a great deal to say about women. Considering the culture in which he lived and taught, a clear picture emerges. Ben Sira was the master of an academy training young Jewish men to become scribes. In an all-male environment, it would be normal for the headmaster to say: "Gentleman, beware of the young ladies. They can cause a lot of trouble for you." Conversely, in an all-female school, it would be commonplace today for the headmistress to say: "Girls, beware of the boys. They can get you into a great deal of trouble." You may have heard something similar when you were a student in school. Or you may have heard a similar warning from your parents or teachers in your adolescence.

The Book of Sirach contains fifty-six verses about women. Twenty-eight verses express positive attributes of women. Twenty-eight verses express negative cautions about women. No one expresses any outrage or concern when the Bible speaks about wicked or evil men. *Deliver me, O Lord, from evil men; preserve me from violent men, who plan evil things in their heart … Guard me O Lord, from the hands of the wicked; preserve me from violent men, who have planned to trip up my feet. Arrogant men have hidden a trap for me* (Psalm 140:1–5). *Incline not my heart to any evil, to busy myself with wicked deeds in company with men who work iniquity* (Psalm 141:4). Few people would give a second thought to the descriptions of the sinful deeds of evil men. No one has a problem talking about evil men or wicked men. Men do not rise up in outrage at those verses.

What about evil women? Are women sacrosanct, above reproach, and free from scrutiny? Are there wicked women who seduce men and betray other women? There are rebellious sons. Are there also rebellious daughters? There are sons who bring shame on their father's good name. Is it fair to speak about daughters who bring disgrace on the good name of the family? Men are guilty of committing the sin of adultery. Does a man commit this sin alone, or is there also a woman involved in the same sinful act? Is Ben Sira prejudiced against women? Is he unfair?

Relationships play an important role in women's lives. Ben Sira frames his positive statements about a woman with respect to her relationships: as wife, mother, or daughter. He contrasts the characteristics of a good wife with the attributes of a bad wife. The same is true in his contrast of a good daughter with a headstrong daughter who brings shame and disgrace to her family. But, with respect to mothers, no comparison is given. A mother deserves honor and respect, simply because God has commanded honor toward parents in His law. Whether she is a good mother or a bad mother is irrelevant. God commands honor for parents.

Two centuries before Christ, the time in which Ben Sira lived, the culture was much different from society today. Girls were seen as more of a burden than a blessing to their parents. Parents would strive to guard a girl's virginity until they could arrange a suitable marriage for her. Should a girl lose her virginity, due to rape or defilement, she would be unacceptable as a bride. A woman was totally dependent upon her father until she married and then she became dependant on her husband. Parents arranged marriages for their daughters based largely on practical considerations. If a wealthy landowner had adjoining property and an unmarried son, that would make a perfect match. A little glimpse into ancient Jewish society can be gleaned from the play *"Fiddler on the Roof."* Tevye the father agreed to a marriage for his eldest daughter with a wealthy widowed butcher, much older than the girl. To his way of thinking, this was a fortunate match.

Moreover, married women could be banished if their husbands found displeasure in them. Consider the story of Michal, Saul's daughter. Michal was given in marriage to David, after he had fought bravely for Israel and for King Saul. But, when Michal criticized David for dancing before the tabernacle of the Lord, David dismissed her from his presence (2 Samuel 6:20–23) and she died childless. Similarly, when Queen Vashti refused to appear before her husband, King Ahasuerus to display her beauty, she was banished from the king's presence forever. Then another queen, Esther, was chosen in her place (Esther 1).

In a time when women were seen as possessions to be transferred from a father to a husband, Ben Sira may be revolutionary in considering a good wife to be a blessing. Rather than being considered a chauvinist, he praises an intelligent wife. Where else in the Bible can you find a woman who is praised for her intelligence? The author of Proverbs praises the ideal wife for her industry, hard work, and concern for the poor. She is enterprising and takes good care of her household. But, there is no mention of her intelligence, nor is she praised as being a blessing.

Ben Sira praises the good wife.
Happy is the husband of a good wife	Sirach 26:1
A good wife is a great blessing	Sirach 26:3
Happy is he who lives with an intelligent wife	Sirach 25:8
Her charm is worth more than gold	Sirach 7:19
A wife's charm delights her husband	Sirach 26:13
A sensible and silent wife is a gift of the Lord	Sirach 26:14

The true revolutionary in advancing the role of women in the Bible is Jesus of Nazareth. Jesus showed honor and respect to His mother. He performed His first miracle at her request (John 2:1–11). Jesus befriended women: *Now Jesus loved Martha and her sister and Lazarus* (John 11:5). Jesus showed compassion to the widow in Nain whose only son had died. Knowing that her security rested in having a son to provide for her, Jesus restored the son to life and gave him back to his mother (Luke 7:11–15). Women were the first to be allowed to witness the evidence of the Resurrection of Christ from the dead on Easter morning.

The feminine genius was recognized and heralded in the Catholic Church by Pope John Paul II. In a Christ-like manner, he welcomed women and children, the sick and the poor, the needy and the marginalized into his presence. He taught the world how to appreciate the giftedness of women, and continued to proclaim the blessing and goodness of virtuous women, much as Ben Sira did.

Woman has a genius all her own, which is vitally essential to both society and the Church …

Without the contribution of women, society is less alive, culture impoverished, and peace less stable. Situations where women are prevented from developing their full potential and from offering the wealth of their gifts should therefore be considered profoundly unjust, not just to women themselves, but to society as a whole …

How many women have been and continue to be valued more for their physical appearance than for their skill, their professionalism, their intellectual abilities, their deep sensitivity; in a word, the very dignity of their being!

I appeal to the whole Church community to be willing to foster feminine participation in every way in its internal life. This is certainly not a new commitment, since it is inspired by the example of Christ himself. Although He chose men as His Apostles—a choice which remains normative for their successors—nevertheless, He also involved women in the cause of His kingdom; indeed He wanted them to be the first witnesses and heralds of His Resurrection.

Pope John Paul II, *The Genius of Women*
(Washington, DC: United States Catholic Conference, 1977), pp. 27, 35, 49

Negative criticisms of women also appear in Sirach. Are the statements objectively true, or is Ben Sira simply a misogynist? Evaluate some negative passages. *From a woman sin had its beginning, and because of her we all die* (Sirach 25:24). This statement obviously refers to original sin (Genesis 3:13), which resulted in the punishment of death for the human race: *to dust you shall return* (Genesis 3:19). Truthfully, the first woman Eve was tempted and sinned, and because of the sin of Adam and Eve, we all do die. All people are implicated in original sin (CCC 402).

Consider the following negative warnings given to the young scribes by Ben Sira:

> *Do not go to meet a loose woman,*
>> *lest you fall into her snares* Sirach 9:3
>
> *Do not give yourself to harlots*
>> *lest you lose your inheritance* Sirach 9:6
>
> *Turn away your eyes from a shapely woman,*
>> *and do not look at beauty belonging to another;*
>> *many have been misled by a woman's beauty* Sirach 9:8
>
> *Never dine with another man's wife,*
>> *nor revel with her at wine* Sirach 9:9

Are these warnings sexist in nature? Or, is this practical wisdom that would protect marriages and family life? Would not men and women be better off if men did not go to meet loose women, did not go to harlots, did not lust after the beauty of another man's wife, and did not wine and dine the wife of another man?

Ben Sira chastises both men and women who break their marriage vows in Sirach 23:18–27. Even though people might conceal the sin of adultery from their spouse or other people, still God sees. Moreover, the children of adulterous relationships experience the disgrace of their parentage.

The wickedness of married men lusting after other women has been objectively described for the young scribes in training. What about the wickedness of evil women? Should the scribes be forewarned about wicked women as well?

> *I would rather dwell with a lion and a dragon*
>> *than dwell with an evil wife* Sirach 25:16
>
> *The wickedness of a wife changes her appearance,*
>> *and darkens her face like that of a bear* Sirach 25:17
>
> *An evil wife is an ox yoke which chafes;*
>> *taking hold of her is like grasping a scorpion* Sirach 26:7
>
> *There is great anger when a wife is drunken;*
>> *she will not hide her shame* Sirach 26:8

Perhaps the most troubling verse in Sirach can be found in Sirach 42:14 *Better is the wickedness of a man than a woman who does good.* This verse illustrates the generic problem in translation issues. Ben Sira wrote in Hebrew. His grandson translated his work into Greek. The Revised Standard Version Catholic Edition (RSVCE) translation comes from the Greek. The literal Hebrew reads: *Better the roughness of a man than a do-gooder woman.* Consider the context of this passage. Immediately preceding this passage, Ben Sira warns parents to keep strict watch over a headstrong daughter, lest she bring shame on the family. Perhaps Ben Sira is still speaking to the parents or guardians of a rebellious daughter. So, the Hebrew translation—Better a man's harshness, than a woman's indulgence—would make perfect sense to parents and guardians. A stern father is often better than an overly indulgent or pampering mother. Wickedness is evil in both men and women. But, good parenting often requires sternness, which can be experienced as harshness for the child. *For the moment all discipline seems painful rather than pleasant; later it yields the peaceful fruit of righteousness to those who have been trained by it* (Hebrews 12:11). Sometimes fathers as well as mothers can be too lax or lenient. In that case, the child is left without anyone to set boundaries, give strong direction and provide firm discipline.

Evidence that Ben Sira is not a misogynist or a hater of women, can be found in the early part of the book, when he speaks of duty to one's parents. *Whoever glorifies his mother is like one who lays up treasure* (Sirach 3:4). Later in the same chapter he says, *It is a disgrace for children not to respect their mother* (Sirach 3:11). So, Ben Sira is advocating that honor and respect be shown to *all* mothers. Whether a mother is good or bad, she is to be honored and respected, simply because she has given the gift of life.

Do not deprive yourself of a wise and good wife, for her charm is worth more than gold (Sirach 7:19). Ben Sira proclaims the goodness of marriage to a wise and good woman in this verse. Moreover, he indicates that the charm of a wise and virtuous wife is worth more than gold. So, although the failings of wicked and evil men and women are discussed clearly and soberly, the virtues of the wise and noble are extolled even more. Wisdom is ascribed to women! Perhaps the final word concerning men and women should be given to Pope Benedict XVI.

When men and women demand to be autonomous and totally self-sufficient, they run the risk of being closed in a self-reliance that considers ignoring every natural, social or religious bond as an expression of freedom, but which in fact, reduces them to an oppressive solitude. To promote and sustain the real advancement of women and men one cannot fail to take this reality into account …

Christianity recognizes and proclaims that men and women share equal dignity and responsibility …

God entrusts to women and men, according to their respective capacities, a specific vocation and mission in the Church and in the world. Here I am thinking of the family, a community of love open to life, the fundamental cell of society. In it the woman and the man, thanks to the gift of maternity and paternity, together carry out an irreplaceable role in regard to life. Children from their conception have the right to be able to count on their father and mother to take care of them and to accompany their growth …

It is necessary to enable the woman to collaborate in the building of society, appreciating her typical "feminine genius."

Pope Benedict XVI, *Address on February 9, 2008*, Clementine Hall.

1. What admonition is given in Sirach 23:13?

2. Identify two sins in the following verses.

Sirach 23:16–21	
Sirach 23:22–27	

3. When and where was wisdom created? Sirach 24:3–9

4. List three things that are beautiful in the sight of God and men. Sirach 25:1

5. List three kinds of people who are found to be offensive. Sirach 25:2

6. Where did sin have its beginning?

Genesis 3:1–20	
Sirach 25:24	
Romans 5:12–21	

7. What can you learn about marriage?

Sirach 7:19	
CCC 1603	
CCC 1604	
CCC 1605	

* Who do you know is an excellent example of a good marriage?

8. Identify some characteristics of a good wife.

Sirach 25:8	
Sirach 26:1–3	
Sirach 26:13–17	

*What characteristics do you think are most important for a good wife?

9. Explain wickedness in women.

Sirach 25:13–17	
Sirach 25:18–26	
Sirach 26:7–12	

* What do you think is the most evil character flaw in a woman?

10. What happens to one who is not steadfast in fearing the Lord? Sirach 27:1–3

11. How are men tested? Sirach 27:4–7

12. Write Sirach 27:9 and Sirach 27:27 as common sayings in your own words.

13. Why should you forgive others? Sirach 28:1–7

14. What has betrayed many virtuous women? Sirach 28:15

15. List three biblical principles about money.

Sirach 29:1–7	
Sirach 29:8–13	
Sirach 29:14–22	

* Have you ever been in a position to lend or to borrow money? How did it feel?

16. What can you learn from these verses?

Sirach 29:23	
Philippians 4:11	

17. What can parents learn from the following verses?

Sirach 30:1–6	
Sirach 30:7–13	

* How would you evaluate your own efforts at discipline?

18. Explain these verses in your own words.

Sirach 31:1–11	
Sirach 31:12–24	
Sirach 31:25–31	

19. Find a common thread in Sirach 31:19 and Sirach 32:14–15.

20. What principles can you learn from Sirach 32:7–9.

Chapter 21

Prayer
Sirach 33–43

O that a guard were set over my mouth,
and a seal of prudence upon my lips,
that it may keep me from falling,
so that my tongue may not destroy me!
O Lord, Father and Ruler of my life,
do not abandon me to their counsel,
and let me not fall because of them!
O that whips were set over my thoughts,
and the discipline of wisdom over my mind!
Sirach 22:27–23:2

Jesus ben Sira not only talks about God to his student scribes, he also prays to God in their hearing and records his prayers. Prayer involves talking to God and listening to God. Every God-seeking person commits himself or herself to daily prayer in some fashion. The prayers of the holy men and women of old serve as an example and model for contemporary prayer. Regular, daily prayer is necessary along with frequent spontaneous prayer to grow in relationship with God.

Prayer, called *euchesthai* in Greek and *precari* in Latin, involves the application of the mind and heart to God as a means of seeking union with Him. Prayer is an act of the virtue of religion, giving deep reverence to God and looking to His divine providence for every human need. God, to whom one prays, moves the soul to prayer. A desire to pray and a spirit of prayer is a gift from God. In order to pray, the individual must first enter into the presence of God, tuning out the distractions of daily life and turning to God. There are four types of prayer, forming the acronym, *ACTS*, each of which should be included in daily prayer.

> **Adoration** — Adore and worship God, because He is worthy of praise.
> **Confession** — Confess personal sins, faults, and omissions.
> **Thanksgiving** — Thank God for all His blessings and graces.
> **Supplication** — Seek and ask from God what you need and desire.

Whether someone is a beginner in prayer, or has been praying for many years, the four basic components of adoration, confession, thanksgiving, and supplication, or intercession help to keep one's prayer life balanced. Children should be taught rote prayers, which can remain in their memories throughout life. They should also be taught how to speak with God personally and intimately. The psalms provide prayers of praise, lamentation, contrition, thanksgiving and intercession. Other places in the Bible offer a window into the prayer life and prayer patterns of individual holy men and women of God.

Six personal prayers of Ben Sira appear in the Book of Sirach, along with many other verses describing the wonders of God and basic characteristics of the wisdom and goodness of God, as he teaches the scribes about Almighty God.

First Prayer	Sirach 22:27–23:6
Second Prayer	Sirach 36:1–22
Third Prayer	Sirach 39:12–35
Fourth Prayer	Sirach 50:22–24
Fifth Prayer	Sirach 51:1–12
Sixth Prayer	Sirach 51:13–30

Ben Sira's fourth prayer is the most brief, and yet includes a prayer of adoration and a prayer of intercession within its three short verses:

> *And now bless the God of all*
> *who in every way does great things;*
> *who exalts our days from birth,*
> *and deals with us according to his mercy.*
> *May he give us gladness of heart,*
> *and grant that peace may be in our days in Israel,*
> *as in the days of old,*
> *that Israel may believe that the God of mercy is with us*
> *to deliver us in our days!*   Sirach 50:22–24

Intercessory prayer characterizes Ben Sira's first prayer, in which he asks God to govern his thoughts, words, and actions. He acknowledges that God is *Lord, Father, and Ruler of my life* (Sirach 23:1). It is uncommon in the Old Testament to find God addressed as *Father*. Sirach appears to be the first writer in the Bible to address God as his Father in such an intimate and personal way. A few hundred years later, Jesus will invite all believers to pray with the familiarity that He enjoys. *"But when you pray, go into your room and shut the door and pray to your Father who is in secret; and your Father who sees in secret will reward you. And in praying, do not heap up empty phrases as the Gentiles do; for they think that they will be heard for their many words. Do not be like them, for your Father knows what you need before you ask him"* (Matthew 6:6–8).

Confession and contrition appear in Ben's Sira's second prayer in Sirach 36. As in a typical prayer of lamentation, the penitent begs for God's mercy and deliverance from his enemies. *"Have mercy upon us, O Lord, the God of all, and look upon us, and show us the light of your mercy; send fear of you upon the nations ... Listen, O Lord, to the prayer of your servants, according to the blessing of Aaron for your people, and direct us in the way of righteousness, and all who are on the earth will know that you are the Lord, the God of the ages* (Sirach 36:1; 36:17).

Sirach 39:12–35 provides a psalm prayer that may be a collective prayer or a combination of prayer to God and teaching to the scribes. In this instance, Ben Sira is not speaking exclusively to God. Rather, he is praising God, while at the same time giving instruction to the students about the majesty and goodness of God. After encouraging a hymn of praise and ascribing majesty to his name, Ben Sira ends this section with "*So now sing praise with all your heart and voice, and bless the name of the Lord* (Sirach 39:35). Prayer is the desire of the soul.

> There is nothing more worthwhile than to pray to God and to converse with him, for prayer unites us with God as his companions. As our bodily eyes are illuminated by seeing the light, so in contemplating God our soul is illuminated by him. ...
>
> Our soul should be directed to God, not merely when we suddenly think of prayer, but even when we are concerned with something else. If we are looking after the poor, if we are busy in some other way, or if we are doing any type of good work, we should season our actions with the desire and the remembrance of God. Through this salt of the love of God we can all become a sweet dish for the Lord. If we are generous in giving time to prayer, we will experience its benefits throughout our life.
>
> Prayer is the light of the soul, giving us true knowledge of God. It is a link mediating between God and man. By prayer the soul is borne up to heaven and in a marvelous way embraces the Lord. This meeting is like that of an infant crying to its mother, and seeking the best of milk. The soul longs for its own needs and what it receives is better than anything to be seen in the world.
>
> Prayer is a precious way of communicating with God; it gladdens the soul and gives repose to its affections. You should not think of prayer as being a matter of words. It is a desire for God, an indescribable devotion, not of human origin, but the gift of God's grace. As Saint Paul says: "We do not know how to pray as we ought, but the Spirit himself intercedes for us with sighs too deep for words" (Romans 8:26).
>
> Saint John Chrysostom (347–407 AD) *Homilies*, 6

A prayer of thanksgiving is offered in Ben Sira's fifth prayer at the beginning of Sirach 51. *I will give thanks to you, O Lord and King, and will praise you as God my Savior ... I will praise your name continually, and will sing praise with thanksgiving. My prayer was heard, for you saved me from destruction and rescued me from an evil plight. Therefore I will give thanks to you and praise you, and I will bless the name of the Lord* (Sirach 51:1, 11–12). Many times people ask God for favors and beg God to deliver them from sickness, financial troubles, relationship problems, or family concerns. They pray and pray and pray to God. But, when God answers and delivers them from the trouble, how many times do they remember to offer thanksgiving to God? If someone begs God for help many, many times, should he thank God only once?

The final prayer of Ben Sira at the end of Sirach 51, is a recounting of his desire for wisdom and a retelling of how he interceded to God in the temple for the gift of wisdom. Even in his recounting, there is a prayer of praise and thanksgiving. *I made progress therein; to him who gives wisdom I will give glory…The Lord gave me a tongue as my reward, and I will praise him with it* (Sirach 51:17, 51:22).

Ben Sira prayed to God for wisdom. *I spread out my hands to the heavens, and lamented my ignorance of her. I directed my soul to her, and through purification I found her* (Sirach 51:19–20). So, the example given to the wisdom seeker is to first recognize a need or deficiency. The proud do not realize their lack. Only the humble turn to God in their need and seek wisdom. Then, expect purification. In order to gain wisdom, one must be purified of the folly and sinfulness that stands in the way of receiving God's gift. Purification involves repentance. The wisdom seeker gets rid of sin and all foolishness, so that he will be an empty vessel for God's wisdom.

In praying and discussing prayer, Ben Sira shares a secret with wisdom seekers. Pope John Paul II proclaimed that the Psalter is an ideal source of Christian prayer and he encouraged lay people to pray the psalms, and enter into the Divine Liturgy. He even invited lay people to pray the Liturgy of the Hours.

> In the Apostolic Letter *Novo Millennio Ineunte* I expressed the hope that the Church would become more and more distinguished in the "art of prayer." …This effort must be expressed above all in the liturgy, the source and summit of ecclesial life. Consequently, it is important to devote greater pastoral care to promoting the *Liturgy of the Hours* as a prayer of the whole People of God.
>
> It is an encouraging fact that many lay people in parishes and ecclesial associations have learned to appreciate it…I would like to encourage and help everyone to pray with the same words that Jesus used, words that for thousands of years have been part of the prayer of Israel and the Church.
>
> We could use various approaches to understanding the Psalms…. consider the various sentiments of the human heart expressed in them: joy, gratitude, thanksgiving, love, tenderness, enthusiasm, but also intense suffering, complaint, pleas for help and for justice, which sometimes lead to anger and imprecation. In the Psalms, the human being fully discovers himself.
>
> John Paul II, *General Audience*, March 28, 2001

Just as Ben Sira demonstrated his prayerfulness, popes, bishops, priests, religious, and lay people in contemporary times demonstrate prayerfulness. The person who begins and ends the day with prayer can accomplish supernatural feats. Even busy people will recognize that they are too busy *not* to pray. Apart from God's blessing, all sorts of additional hassles and obstacles present themselves. Soaked in prayer, a person can accomplish far more than ever imagined. In whatever form or manner, the wisdom seeker must set aside time every day for prayer. Turn off the television and the radio. Step away from the computer and the telephone. Find a quite place and put your heart in God's hands. Speak to Him and then listen. Let God speak to you and listen to Him. Prayer can transform your life.

Before you speak, it is necessary for you to listen, for God speaks in the silence of the heart. Give yourself fully to God. He will use you to accomplish great things on the condition that you believe much more in His love than in your own weakness.

Sweetest Lord, make me appreciative of the dignity of my high vocation, and its many responsibilities. Never permit me to disgrace it by giving way to coldness, unkindness, or impatience.

We need to find God, and He cannot be found in noise and restlessness. God is the friend of silence. See how nature—trees, flowers, grass—grows in silence; see the stars, the moon and the sun, how they move in silence … We need silence to be able to touch souls.

Keep the joy of loving God in your heart and share this joy with all you meet especially your family. Be holy.

A sacrifice to be real must cost, must hurt, and must empty ourselves. The fruit of silence is prayer, the fruit of prayer is faith, the fruit of faith is love, the fruit of love is service, and the fruit of service is peace.

Blessed Teresa of Calcutta (1910–1997)

1. What two themes does Ben Sira revisit in Sirach 33:1–2?

2. For whom did Ben Sira write his book? Sirach 33:17

3. Identify a source of "An idle mind is the devil's workshop." Sirach 33:27–28

4. How should a wisdom seeker think about dreams? Sirach 34:1–8

5. Identify a source of education, apart from school, in Sirach 34:11.

* What have you learned from travel?

6. Describe one who "fears of the Lord." Sirach 34:13–17

7. Put these instructions in your own words.

Sirach 35:1–2	
Sirach 35:3	
Sirach 35:4–7	
Sirach 35:8–11	

8. Write two favorite verses from the prayer in Sirach 36:1–17.

* Now write your own short prayer of petition to God.

* When and how do you pray each day?

9. Write a positive assessment of a woman from Sirach 36:22–24.

10. What is the lot of the bachelor? Sirach 36:25

11. How should a person make a moral decision? Sirach 37:14–15

12. What can you learn about moral decisions and virtue?

Sirach 37:27–31	
CCC 1776	
CCC 1777	
CCC 1778	
CCC 1798	

* How would you know if you have a well-formed conscience?

13. Explain Sirach 38:1–15.

14. What advice is given in Sirach 38:16–23?

* Have you mourned appropriately or excessively for deceased loved ones? Explain.

15. How are the people who work with their hands esteemed? Sirach 38:25–34

16. Explain the role of the scribe.

Sirach 38:24	
Sirach 39:1–3	
Sirach 39:4	
Sirach 39:5	
Sirach 39:6–8	
Sirach 39:9–10	
Sirach 39:11	

* The scribe will leave a name for himself. How would you like to be remembered?

17. Choose two favorite verses from Sirach 40 and tell why you chose them.

18. What can you learn about death?

Sirach 41:1–4	
Sirach 41:10	
Sirach 41:11–13	

19. List two shameful things and two opposite things. Sirach 41:17–42:8

20. Choose five marvels of God's creation from Sirach 42:15–43:33.

* What is the relationship between God and His works? CCC 300, Sirach 43:28

CHAPTER 22

Israel's Heroes
Sirach 44–51

Let us now praise famous men,
and our fathers in their generations.
The Lord apportioned to them great glory,
his majesty from the beginning.
Sirach 44:1–2

he Chosen People were displaced from the Promised Land in the course of their history. How can a people maintain their identity and their culture when they are banished from their land or sent into captivity, as in the Babylonian exile? How can a people remain faithful to God and transmit their culture to the young when they are uprooted or new cultures compete for their allegiance? This was a problem facing the Jewish people, and perhaps a problem that weighed heavily on the heart of Ben Sira. Land, language, and religion help to keep a culture intact. In contemporary times, Poland has been devastated time and again. It has been said that in World War II, Poland lost the war twice: once to the Germans and then to the Russians. Their language, their culture, and their Catholic faith kept Poland alive.

Heroes are people of uncommon valor. They demonstrate extraordinary character, which can be emulated by others. In every culture, young people look for courageous examples to take as role models. The wisdom teacher points out several excellent examples of famous people who have brought glory to God and honor to their people. God's glory illuminates through the lives of Israel's godly ancestors.

At this point in salvation history, there is not yet a well-developed understanding of the after-life. Ben Sira, therefore, explains that even after their death, godly people will be remembered by their children, and a good name will continue to be respected for generations to come.

But these were men of mercy,
        whose righteous deeds have not been forgotten;
their prosperity will remain with their descendants,
        and their inheritance to their children's children.
Their descendants stand by the covenants;
        their children also, for their sake.
Their posterity will continue for ever,
        and their glory will not be blotted out.
Their bodies were buried in peace,
        and their name lives to all generations.
Peoples will declare their wisdom,
        and the congregation proclaims their praise. Sirach 44:10–15

Interestingly, Ben Sira begins his account of the heroes of Israel with Enoch. Enoch was the father of Methuselah. *Enoch walked with God; and he was not, for God took him* (Genesis 5:24). Adam and Eve walked with God in the Garden of Eden, and they talked with God intimately. But, after the fall into sin and the expulsion from the garden, people were distant from God. But Enoch walked with God and then he disappeared. God took him, but there is no evidence that Enoch died. This mysterious transfer of a believer to heaven without experiencing death provided a fascinating example for wisdom seekers to ponder.

Noah was a righteous man, blameless in his generation; Noah walked with God (Genesis 6:9). Because Noah was a righteous man and blameless in God's sight, God established His covenant with Noah. In God's covenant with Noah, He placed the rainbow in the sky as a sign, and promised never again to destroy all living things by means of a flood. Ben Sira describes Noah as being *found perfect and righteous* (Sirach 44:17).

The Patriarchs — Ben Sira praises Abraham because *Abraham was the great father of a multitude of nations, and no one has been found like him in glory; he kept the law of the Most High* (Sirach 44:19–20). Remember that God did not give the law to Moses on Mount Sinai until long after Abraham had died. And yet, God inscribed His law on the hearts of men. Something in the conscience of man reveals right and wrong. God's promise of progeny to Abraham was fulfilled in Isaac (Sirach 44:22) and Jacob and his sons (Sirach 44:23).

Ben Sira describes Moses as a man of mercy, who was beloved by God and man, and whose memory is blessed (Sirach 45:1). He alludes to the plagues and the wonders of the Exodus as a means by which God was glorified through Moses, the miracle worker. God gave Moses the commandments and revealed His glory to him. God sanctified Moses through faithfulness and meekness (Sirach 45:3–4).

Extensive coverage is given to Aaron, the priest, the brother of Moses. *He exalted Aaron, the brother of Moses, a holy man like him, of the tribe of Levi. ... Moses ordained him, and anointed him with holy oil* (Sirach 45:6, 45:15). This lengthy treatment of Aaron (Sirach 45:6–22) prepares the wisdom seeker for the climax of the retelling of Israel's heroes with the praise of Simon the high priest in Sirach 50:1–24. The esteem in which Ben Sira holds the priesthood and the liturgical functions of the priest emerges clearly.

Joshua, Caleb, Judges, and Samuel receive praise in Sirach 46. Joshua succeeded Moses in leading the Chosen People into the Promised Land. Ben Sira recounts that, *Joshua the son of Nun was mighty in war, and was the successor of Moses in prophesying* (Sirach 46:1). Moses sent Joshua and Caleb as spies into the Promised Land. They found it to be a land flowing with milk and honey. Joshua and Caleb sensed God's favor and wanted to go in and take the land. But others were fearful (Numbers 13–14). Joshua's military exploits are recounted in Joshua 1–11. Ben Sira only praises those judges who did not fall into idolatry. Samuel, beloved of the Lord, is recalled as a prophet, judge, and priest.

Prophets and kings — Ben Sira retells the life of David in very favorable terms. He recalls David's early life as a shepherd. When David was still a youth, he slew Goliath the giant, taking away the reproach from the people. Later he wiped out his enemies on every side. *"In all that he did he gave thanks to the Holy One, the Most High, with ascriptions of glory; he sang praise with all his heart, and he loved his Maker* (Sirach 47:8). David's sins against Uriah the Hittite and his wife Bathsheba are not recounted in Sirach (2 Samuel 11). Rather it simply says, *The Lord took away his sins, and exalted his power for ever; he gave him the covenant of kings and a throne of glory in Israel* (Sirach 47:11).

Following David, a wise son, Solomon reigned in a time of peace and built the Temple in Jerusalem, where later the priests would minister before the Lord. Although Solomon was wise in his youth and amassed silver and gold, the sin of his adult life is clearly reported here. *But you laid your loins beside women, and through your body you were brought into subjection. You put stain upon your honor, and defiled your posterity, so that you brought wrath upon your children and they were grieved at your folly* (Sirach 47:19–20). Note the contrast between the wisdom of Solomon's youth and the folly of his later years. Recall the earlier passage: *My soul hates three kinds of men, and I am greatly offended at their life: a beggar who is proud, a rich man who is a liar, and an adulterous old man who lacks good sense* (Sirach 25:2).

Elijah, Elisha, and Hezekiah appear in Sirach 48. *How glorious you were, O Elijah, in your wondrous deeds! And who has the right to boast which you have? You who raised a corpse from death and from Hades, by the word of the Most High.* (Sirach 48:4–5). Elijah had restored to life the dead son of the widow at Zarephath, who had offered him hospitality (1 Kings 17:10–24). Elijah did not die, but was taken up into heaven by horses and a chariot of fire in a whirlwind (2 Kings 2:11), and is recalled in Sirach 48:9.

Elisha asked for a double portion of the spirit of his mentor, Elijah. *Elisha was filled with his spirit. … Nothing was too hard for him, and when he was dead his body prophesied. As in his life he did wonders, so in death his deeds were marvelous* (Sirach 48:12–14). The amazing events in the life of the prophet Elisha are recorded in detail in 2 Kings 2–13. Ben Sira gives a brief summary here.

After praising Hezekiah for doing what was pleasing in the sight of the Lord and Josiah who took away the abominations of iniquity and led the people aright, Ben Sira moves on to discuss Ezekiel. *It was Ezekiel who saw the vision of glory which God showed him above the chariot of the cherubim. For God remembered his enemies with storm, and did good to those who directed their ways rightly* (Sirach 49:8–9).

The high point of the parade of Israel's heroes appears in Simon the high priest. Simon, or Simeon II, son of Onias (Jochanan) was the high priest in the Temple in Jerusalem from 219 to 196 BC. According to the historian Josephus, Simon renovated the Temple and fortified its precincts. The pinnacle of this section is the description of Simon presiding at a Temple liturgy. *How glorious he was when the people gathered around him as he came out of the inner sanctuary!* (Sirach 50:5). Eleven similes in Sirach 50:6–10 illustrate the glorious appearance of the high priest. The description of the robes of the high priest recalls the explanation of Aaron's vestments in Sirach 45:6–13.

Interestingly, *And now bless the God of all, who in every way does great things; who exalts our days from birth, and deals with us according to his mercy* (Sirach 50:22) appears in several contemporary hymns and songs of praise. Consider the hymn "Now Thank We All Our God" which derives from this verse.

Finally, the book ends with a personal signature and prayer. It is uncommon in the Old Testament for an author to refer to himself in the first person. Rarely do authors identify themselves. But, a grandson translator identifies Ben Sira in the prologue and then Ben Sira identifies himself in Sirach 50:

> *Instruction in understanding and knowledge*
> *I have written in this book,*
> *Jesus the son of Sirach, son of Eleazar, of Jerusalem,*
> *who out of his heart poured forth wisdom.*
> *Blessed is he who concerns himself with these things,*
> *and he who lays them to heart will become wise.*
> *For if he does them, he will be strong for all things,*
> *for the light of the Lord is his path.*
> Sirach 50:27–29

Ben Sira offers a hymn of thanksgiving to God, in which he relates events in his personal life that he wishes to share. The hymn of thanksgiving follows the traditional pattern of psalms of thanksgiving.

Invocation of God	Sirach 51:1
Reasons for giving thanks	Sirach 51:2–5
Prayer for deliverance	Sirach 51:6–10
Praise for God's response	Sirach 51:11–12

Then, the wisdom teacher turns his attention back to his students, and once again advises them to seek wisdom. Wisdom is better than silver and gold. Wisdom enables the student to praise God and rejoice in His mercy. In His time, God will reward the wisdom seeker for his efforts. The One who gives wisdom is worthy of glory and honor and praise. Ben Sira has shown that men and women, young and old, can seek after and attain wisdom. Becoming the best person that God has created you to be brings glory to God. Ask God for wisdom. Seek wisdom and you will become wise, by God's grace. Bible study is a perfect means of seeking God, growing in wisdom, and conforming your life to God's Law. So keep up the good wook and press on.

Wisdom is a sharing in God's ability to see and judge things as they really are. God reveals himself as God by his just judgments; as God, he sees things without disguise, as they really are, and deals with each according to his truth. Wisdom is a sharing in God's way of seeing reality. ... We cannot possess it unless we are united with God ... Only if we let ourselves be cleansed of the corruptibility of the "I" and come thus gradually to live by God, to be united with God, do we come to a true inner freedom of judgment, to a fearless independence of thinking and deciding, that no longer cares about the approval or disapproval of others but clings only to truth. Such a purification is always a process of opening oneself and, at the same time, of receiving oneself.

Pope Benedict XVI, (Joseph Cardinal Ratzinger), *Principles of Catholic Theology*,
Translated by Sister Mary Frances McCarthy S.N.D.
(San Francisco: Ignatius Press, 1987), p. 357

1. What kinds of people are praised in Sirach 44:1–15?

2. Describe something praiseworthy about the following men.

Enoch	Sirach 44:16
Noah	Sirach 44:17–18
Abraham	Sirach 44:19–21
Isaac	Sirach 44:22
Jacob	Sirach 44:23

3. What virtue is praised in Moses?

Sirach 45:4	
CCC 716	

* Describe a person you know who is humble and meek.

4. Describe some characteristics of Aaron. Sirach 45:6–22

5. What is praiseworthy about Phinehas? Sirach 45:23–24

6. List some positive traits of Joshua and Caleb. Sirach 46:1–12

7. What is notable about Samuel? Sirach 46:13–20

8. What can you learn about David?

Sirach 47:2	
Sirach 47:3–5	
Sirach 47:6–7	
Sirach 47:8–10	
Sirach 47:11	

9. Describe some positive and negative attributes of Solomon.

Sirach 47:12–13	
Sirach 47:14–18	
Sirach 47:19–22	

10. Describe Solomon's sons. Sirach 47:23–25

* Who is the wisest person you know? To whom would you go for advice?

11. What can you learn about Elijah?

Sirach 48:1	
CCC 696	
Sirach 48:2–8	
Sirach 48:9–10	

12. Describe Elisha and Hezekiah.

Sirach 48:12–16	
Sirach 48:17–25	

13. From Sirach 49, write something about the following heroes of faith.

Josiah	
Ezekiel	
Nehemiah	
Enoch	
Joseph	

14. What is praiseworthy about Simon? Sirach 50:1–21

15. Paraphrase the prayer found in Sirach 50:22–24.

16. What autobiographical information can you glean in Sirach 50:27?

17. What can you learn about Ben Sira from his prayer in Sirach 51:1–12?

18. When did Ben Sira seek wisdom? Sirach 51:13–22

19. What extracurricular educational activity did Ben Sira enjoy? Sirach 51:13

20. What final advice is given in Sirach 51:23–30?

* Who are your heroes in the faith? List three and describe them.

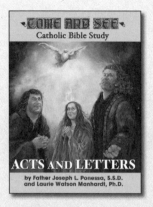
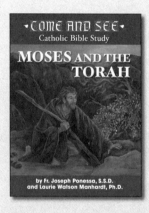
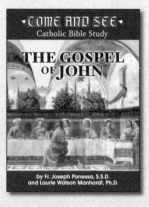
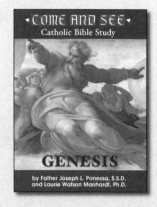
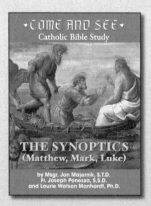
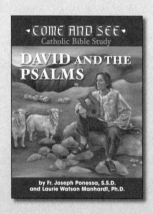
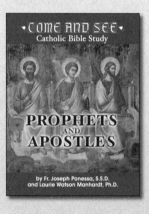

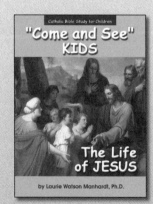

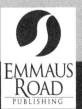